TROMBONE

BY MATTHEW SHEPHARD

PLAYBACK+
Speed • Pitch • Balance • Loop

To access audio and video visit:
www.halleonard.com/mylibrary

Enter Code
2579-5443-0643-1171

ISBN 978-1-70510-266-4

HAL•LEONARD®

Copyright © 2022 by HAL LEONARD LLC
International Copyright Secured All Rights Reserved

No part of this publication may be reproduced in any form or by
any means without the prior written permission of the Publisher.

Visit Hal Leonard Online at
www.halleonard.com

| Contact us:
Hal Leonard
7777 West Bluemound Road
Milwaukee, WI 53213
Email: info@halleonard.com | In Europe, contact:
Hal Leonard Europe Limited
42 Wigmore Street
Marylebone, London, W1U 2RN
Email: info@halleonardeurope.com | In Australia, contact:
Hal Leonard Australia Pty. Ltd.
4 Lentara Court
Cheltenham, Victoria, 3192 Australia
Email: info@halleonard.com.au |

4	**INTRODUCTION**
5	**LESSON 1** Assembly and Instrument Care
9	**LESSON 2** Mouthpiece Buzzing
11	**LESSON 3** Understanding Music
12	**LESSON 4** Long Tones
16	**LESSON 5** Reading Notes
49	**LESSON 6** Syncopation
58	**LESSON 7** Articulations
79	**LESSON 8** Vibrato
83	**LESSON 9** Lip Slurs
109	**LESSON 10** Common Time and Cut Time
126	Alternate Positions
127	Vocabulary Terms
128	Position Chart

89	Addams Family Theme	60	The Banana Boat Song	68	Colors of the Wind
65	All About That Bass	51	Blister in the Sun	102	Danny Boy
38	All My Loving	27	Blowin' in the Wind	65	Danse Bacchanale
97	All Star	21	Boil Them Cabbage Down	119	Do Nothin' Till You Hear from Me
121	All You Need Is Love	98	Bridal Chorus	55	Don't Know Why
25	Allegro ("Spring")	57	Can Can	105	Don't Stop Believin'
95	Another One Bites the Dust	39	Can You Feel The Love Tonight	36	Eight Days a Week
64	Apache	108	Can't Help Falling in Love	92	Eine Kleine Nachtmusik ("Serenade"), First Movement Excerpt
46	Aquarius	33	Carnival of Venice		
42	Arirang	99	Centerfold	23	Every Breath You Take
52	Bad, Bad Leroy Brown	76	Chariots of Fire	98	Eye of the Tiger
63	Bad Medicine	30	Chiapanecas	41	Fields of Gold
31	Bad Romance				

Page	Title
51	Fireflies
40	Firework
44	Forrest Gump - Main Title (Feather Theme)
21	Frère Jacques (Are You Sleeping?)
98	Funeral March
120	Georgia on My Mind
58	Ghostbusters
94	Give Me That Old Time Religion
95	The Good, The Bad and The Ugly (Main Title)
118	Habanera
26	Hallelujah Chorus
57	Happy Together
117	Here's That Rainy Day
122	Hey Jude
53	Hey, Soul Sister
109	I Heard It Through the Grapevine
32	I Just Can't Wait to Be King
22	I Love Rock 'N Roll
102	I Still Haven't Found What I'm Looking For
100	I Wish
76	I'll Be There
44	I'm a Believer
99	If You're Happy and You Know It
112	Imagine
74	In The Hall of the Mountain King
39	Into the Unknown
71	Iron Man
35	Isn't She Lovely
71	It Don't Mean a Thing (If It Ain't Got That Swing)
88	Itsy Bitsy Spider
29	Theme From "Jaws"
19	Jingle Bells
37	Joy to the World
46	Jupiter
47	Theme from "Jurassic Park"
59	Karma Chameleon
34	Largo
29,49	Lean on Me
64	Linus and Lucy
82	The Lion Sleeps Tonight
63	Livin' on a Prayer
20	London Bridge
20	The Longest Time
18	Love Me Tender
21	Love Story
96	Lullaby
59	The Magnificent Seven
48	Maneater
115	March (from the Nutcracker)
28	The Medallion Calls
18	Merrily We Roll Along
35	Mickey Mouse March
49	Minuet in G Major
38	Mr. Tambourine Man
43	Moon River
72	More Than Words
25	Morning
74	Morning Has Broken
45	My Favorite Things
34	My Girl
20	My Heart Will Go On (Love Theme From 'Titanic')
20	Nobody Knows the Trouble I've Seen
50	Nowhere Man
19	Ode to Joy
66	Oh, Pretty Woman
62	Old Time Rock & Roll
42	On Top of Old Smoky
29	Open Arms
103	Over the Rainbow
92	Oye Como Va
24	Part of Your World
91	Perfect
26	Piano Man
103	Polka Dots and Moonbeams
125	Pomp And Circumstance
18	Rain, Rain Go Away
77	Raindrops Keep Fallin' on My Head
56	Right Here Waiting
35	Rosanna
88	Row, Row, Row Your Boat
32	Secrets
75	Seven Nation Army
43	She Drives Me Crazy
22	Shepherd's Hey
61	Shut Up and Dance
22	The Siamese Cat Song
47	(Sittin' On) The Dock of the Bay
71	Smoke on the Water
80	Somewhere Out There
97	Spinning Song
75	SpongeBob SquarePants Theme Song
66	Stand By Me
114	The Star-Spangled Banner
106	Strangers in the Night
70	Summertime
58	Sunshine of Your Love
78	Sweet Caroline
116	Sweet Home Alabama
124	Symphony No. 5 In C Minor, First Movement Excerpt
60	Tainted Love
119	Take Me Out to the Ball Game
54	Take on Me
107	Tears in Heaven
101	That's Amoré (That's Love)
61	This Is Halloween
123	Time in a Bottle
110	Tomorrow
27	True Colors
18	Trumpet Voluntary
47	25 or 6 to 4
93	Unchained Melody
96	Under Pressure
68	Under The Bridge
81	Unforgettable
23	The Victors (Michigan Fight Song)
96	Walk This Way
77	The Wanderer
73	The Way You Look Tonight
22	We Are Family
48	We Found Love
94	We're Not Gonna Take It
69	When The Saints Go Marching In
31	William Tell Overture
104	Wonderful Tonight
54	Yeah!
67	Yesterday
90	You and Me
50	You Are the Sunshine of My Life
111	You've Got a Friend
113	You've Got a Friend in Me

INTRODUCTION

Welcome to *Do It Yourself Trombone*! This book is designed for adults and older beginners who are learning to play the trombone for the first time. You will be taken step by step through the process of learning a new instrument: from the assembling the trombone, to reading notes, and finally playing many songs you have heard on the radio, in movies and on television! It may be tempting to jump around in the book to your favorite pieces, but each page progresses forward by building upon the previous songs and lessons.

There are over 160 songs that reinforce topics covered throughout this book. Whether your favorite genre is rock, pop, jazz, classical, country, rap, musical and movie soundtracks or others, there are many songs you'll recognize and enjoy learning to play. In addition to exercises and songs, there are "Toolboxes" throughout this book that introduce new concepts as you embark on this DIY journey. You will also find several "Trombone Talk" boxes that address concepts and strategies specific to your new instrument.

On page 1, you will find a unique code. Go to **www.halleonard.com/mylibrary** and enter that code to give access to audio and video online, for download or streaming. There you will find expert video instruction to get you started on the right foot, plus video and audio demonstration of many songs found in this book. These spots are indicated throughout the book by these symbols: ▶ 🔊

It also includes PLAYBACK+, a multi-functional audio player that allows you to slow down audio without changing pitch, set loop points, and pan left or right—available exclusively from Hal Leonard.

Learning to play the trombone can be a fulfilling hobby or a serious pursuit. Either way, it is a highly rewarding experience. Whatever your goals, we hope you enjoy the journey and discover the fun of playing the trombone.

About the Author

Matthew Shephard serves as the Director of Bands at Meridian (Michigan) Public Schools. He attended Central Michigan University, where he earned both his Bachelor of Music Education and Master of Music in Conducting degrees. Mr. Shephard has led his Jr. High and High School ensembles to consistent superior ratings at both Michigan School Band & Orchestra Association (MSBOA) District and State Festivals. Under his leadership, the high school band has grown to well over 120 musicians, which represents over one-third of the student population. The Symphonic Band is a frequent performer at the Michigan Music Conference, and his jazz bands have been featured annually at the Detroit Jazz Festival since 2012. Mr. Shephard has been honored in 2018 and 2019 as a Grammy® Music Educator of the Year quarterfinalist and in 2022 as a semifinalist. Mr. Shephard has served on the MSBOA State Executive Board as President. He and his wife Abby have three boys, Aiden, Jonah and Keegan.

LESSON 1:
Assembly & Instrument Care

Parts of the Trombone

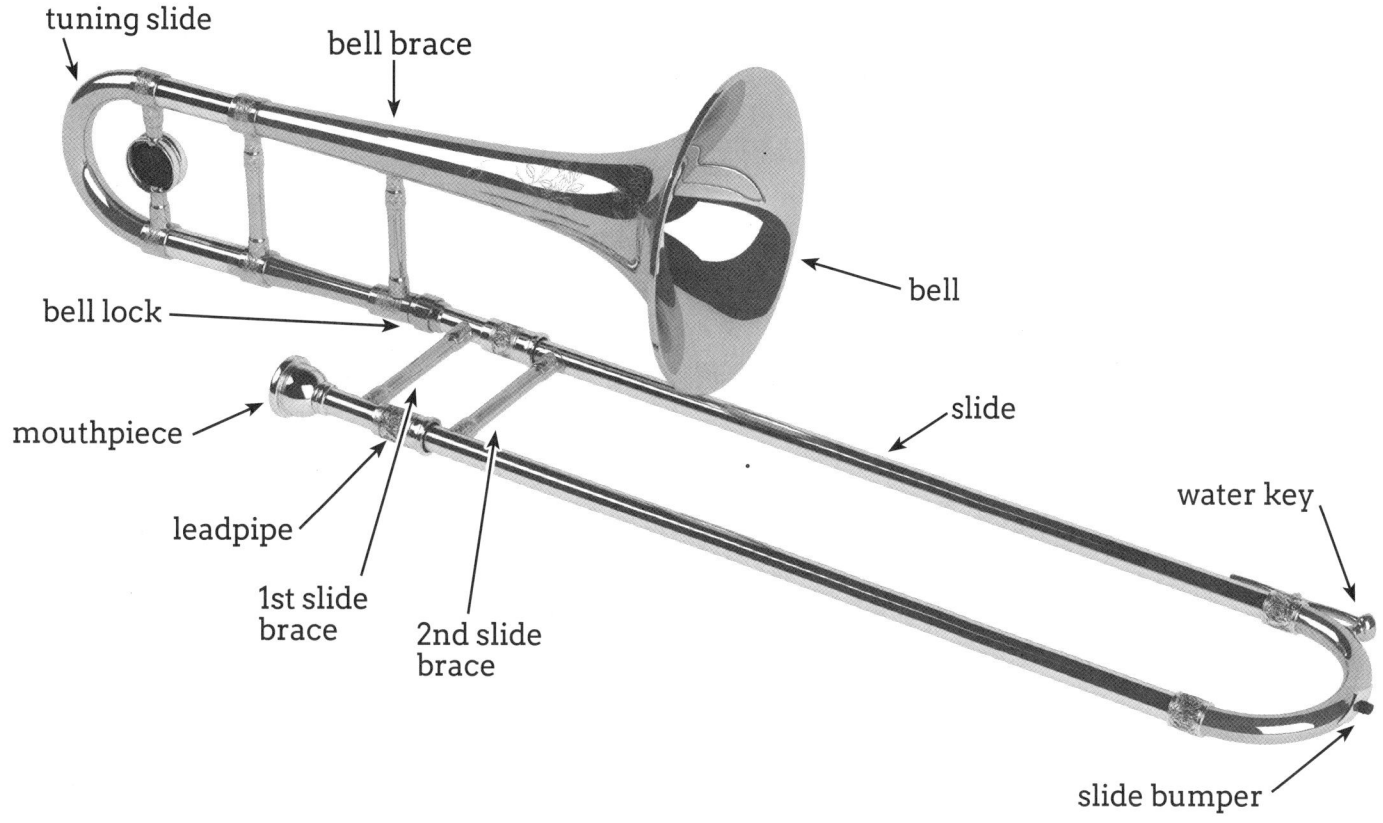

ASSEMBLING YOUR TROMBONE

ALWAYS begin with the slide!

1. The slide should be placed vertically with the ground, resting on the slide bumper. Verify your slide is locked, placing the slide between your legs.

2. Place the bell piece on the threaded end of the slide, making a 90° angle between the bell and the slide. The bell should be resting at 9 o'clock and the leadpipe of the slide is at 12 o'clock.

3. Place the mouthpiece in the leadpipe and give a slight twist to lock it securely. DO NOT push the mouthpiece into place with your hand.

TROMBONE HAND POSITION

MAKE SURE YOUR SLIDE IS LOCKED!

LEFT HAND:

1. Make a gun with your left hand.

2. Your thumb will wrap over the bell brace. If you have a trombone equipped with an F attachment, your thumb will be placed on the trigger.

3. Place your pointer finger on the mouthpiece base, keeping your gun formation from earlier.

4. The remaining fingers will wrap around the bottom tube of the slide between the first and second slide braces.

RIGHT HAND:

1. Split your right hand fingers between the middle and ring fingers to form a "V."

2. Hold the second slide brace between your thumb and first two fingers. Your ring and pinky fingers will rest below the bottom slide, next to your top fingers.

HOLDING THE TROMBONE

When your trombone is in the playing position, the bell piece will be resting on your left shoulder. Bring the mouthpiece to your lips, unlock the slide, and place your right hand on the slide as described. The movement of the slide is led by your wrist, not your elbow, allowing you to move the slide quickly and smoothly. Your right hand palm should be aimed toward the ground, not your face when moving the slide.

LUBRICATING THE SLIDE

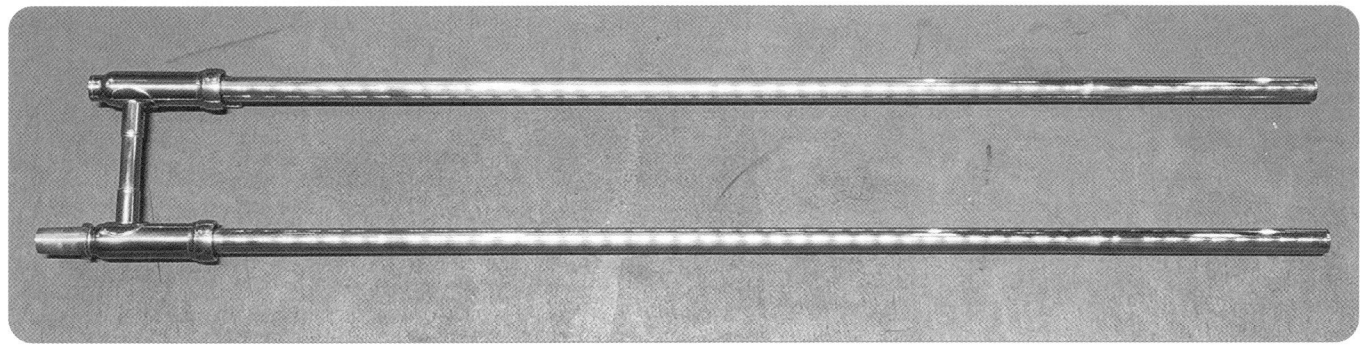

Carefully remove the outer slide and place it in your trombone case. If the inner or outer slides bump against a chair, music stand or another object, your slide will be bent and will not move freely.

 If using slide oil:
1. The inner slide receives two drops of oil on both stems at both 2nd position and 6th position.
2. When placing the inner slide back in the outer casing, avoid putting it in on an angle. This will bend the slide.
3. Carefully place the outer slide over the inner slide and "work in" the oil. Note the placement of the water key and slide lock. It must be on the correct way!

> **TOOLBOX**
>
> **SLIDE SAFETY**
> Always lock your slide when you are not playing the trombone. This will keep your slide straight and moving freely.

 If using slide cream (preferred):
1. Place a very small amount of cream on both stems at both 2nd position and 6th position.
2. Spread cream evenly across the slide by hand, and give the inner slide a few sprays of water from a small bottle.
3. When placing the inner slide back in the outer casing, avoid putting it in on an angle. This will bend the slide.
4. Carefully place the outer slide over the inner slide and "work in" the cream. Note the placement of the water key and slide lock. It must be on the correct way!

You should only need to oil your slide once per week as long as it is in good playing condition. If you are using slide cream, the slide will stay well lubricated for several weeks. A small spray of water each day will activate the cream and make your slide smooth while playing. DO NOT mix oil and cream as this will create a vacuum between your inner and outer slide. If you decide to use different creams or oils, always clean your slide completely before applying the new product.

TUNING SLIDE

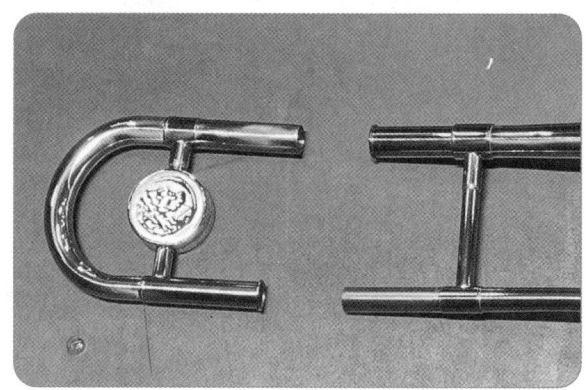

1. Remove the top tuning slide (located near the weight on the bell piece).
2. Place a small amount of tuning slide grease on each tube, then work the grease into the bell piece one side at a time.
3. Carefully place the greased tuning slide back into the trombone, avoiding pushing the slide into the bell piece on an angle.

CLEANING YOUR TROMBONE

TOOLS NEEDED
- Mouthpiece brush
- Vinyl slide snake

- All slides should be oiled/greased regularly.
- Mouthpiece should be cleaned weekly with soap and warm water. You can purchase a mouthpiece brush to scrub the inside of your mouthpiece if desired.
- Give your instrument a bath a few times each year.
  - Take the outer and inner slide apart and place in a bathtub with the bell.
  - Soak the trombone pieces in warm water. No soap should be used!
  - Scrub out the inner and outer slide with a trombone snake (often found in trombone cleaning kits).
  - Rinse out the inner and outer slide with water after scrubbing out residue.
  - Towel dry the trombone.
  - Repeat the tuning slide grease routine once the instrument is dry.

EMPTYING THE WATER KEY

Make sure the water key (also referred to as spit valve) is on the lower outer slide of the trombone. This allows the water to drain from the slide and be emptied easily.

When your instrument makes a gurgling sound, there is water inside your trombone. To empty the water out of the slide:

1. Lock the trombone slide
2. Push water key release valve
3. Blow air into the leadpipe (or mouthpiece if attached). Avoid buzzing when blowing into the instrument to empty the water.

LESSON 2:
Mouthpiece Buzzing

Buzzing in the mouthpiece is what creates the sound on your instrument. If you can manipulate your lips and air stream to make different sounds on the mouthpiece, you will be able to produce many different notes on your instrument. The position of your mouth on the mouthpiece is called your **embouchure**.

1. Take a deep breath and gently place your lips together. Blow the air out of your lips, which will cause them to flap together like you are making a "horse" sound.
2. Moisten your lips and bring them together as if you are saying "mmm."
3. Drop your lower jaw slightly to allow a gap between bottom and top teeth.
4. Pull back the corners of your mouth to create a slight smile.
5. Set the mouthpiece against your lips without placing the lips "inside" the mouthpiece.
6. The mouthpiece should be centered on your lips, with slightly more mouthpiece on the upper lip.
7. Take a full breath from the corners of your mouth, not moving the mouthpiece off your face.
8. Start your buzz by moving your tongue as if you were saying "ta." Your tongue will touch your upper teeth.
9. Blow the airstream through the center of the mouthpiece to create a buzz.
10. Keep the center of your lips relaxed while the corners of your mouth are firm when you buzz in the mouthpiece.

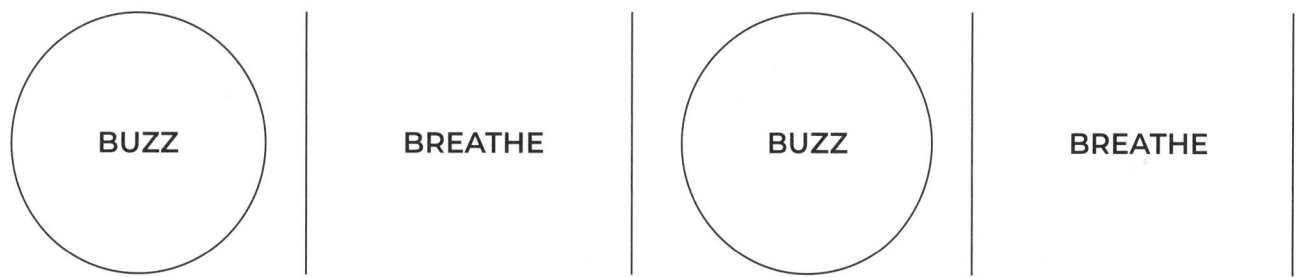

Place your finger between your top and bottom molars. Keep this open feeling in your mouth when you are playing. The inside of your mouth should be shaped as if an egg was placed on your tongue. The proper shape inside your mouth will help in producing a good sound on your instrument. This is called your **tone**. Your tone should be **dark** as if you were saying the word "oh." If your throat is tightened and your top and bottom teeth are together, your tone will be pinched and **bright**, like you were saying "eee." Keep your throat relaxed like when you yawn, and use lots of air. It is *VITAL* that you use lots of air and keep your throat as relaxed as possible!

Buzz four sounds on your mouthpiece. Remember to keep your throat relaxed and your top and bottom teeth apart. Start each buzz as if you were saying the word "ta."

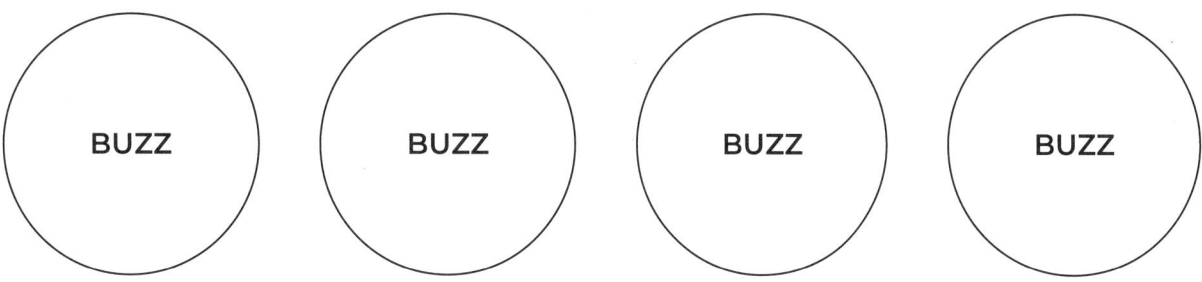

To make the pitch sound lower, you must loosen your lips. Imagine that you are blowing bubbles in a large glass of water, or making an engine sound in the water while swimming in a pool. This is what your lips will feel like when you are trying to play notes that are low. The air must be supported, but your lips will not be pushed together very tightly.

When you want the pitch to sound higher, you must tighten the center of your lips. This causes the air to escape from a much smaller hole. This smaller surface area for the air to escape causes more pressure to be built, making the note sound higher. In addition, you need the air speed to be fast as it enters the mouthpiece to make these higher pitches. Your airstream should be pointed down toward the bottom of the mouthpiece when trying to play higher.

Note: If you have lips that are fuller, you may have to roll some of your upper and lower lip inward toward your teeth to decrease the amount of lip resting against the mouthpiece. Think of this like trying to kiss your teeth.

The opening that the air leaves your mouth and enters the mouthpieces is called the **aperture**. The size of the aperture will determine whether the note is high or low.

BUZZING EXERCISES:

***Always** start your buzz by moving your tongue as if you were saying "ta." Your tongue will touch your upper teeth.*

1. Try buzzing a pitch that lasts for five seconds. Did you run out of air?
2. Make a low sound while buzzing on your mouthpiece.
3. Make a high sound while buzzing on your mouthpiece.
4. Start buzzing a low sound and tighten your lips to gradually make a higher sound. *When you tighten your lips, your aperture is getting smaller.*
5. Start buzzing a high sound and loosen your lips to gradually make a lower sound.
6. Make siren sounds by buzzing from low to high, then back to low. Do this all in one big breath.

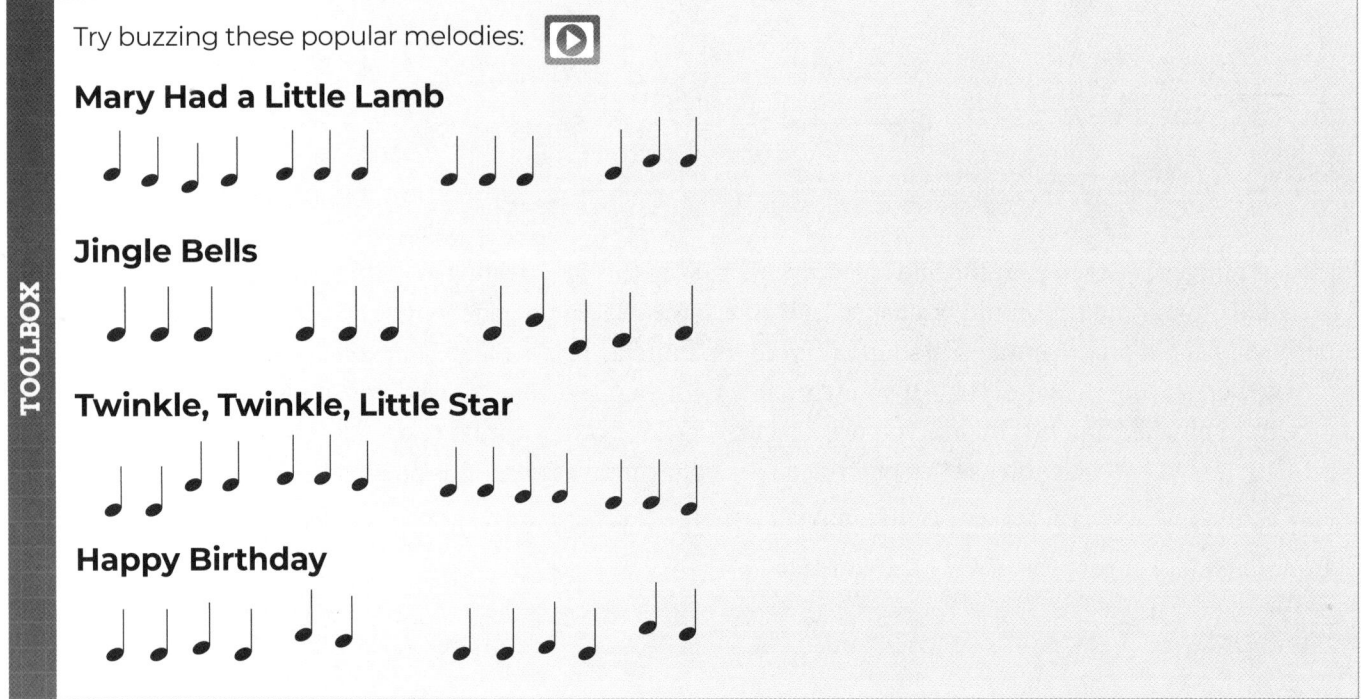

LESSON 3:
Understanding Music

The Staff
Five lines and four spaces where music is written.

Ledger Lines
Lines that extend the music staff higher and lower.

Bar Line
Divides the music staff into measures.

Bar Line

Measure
The space between two bar lines.

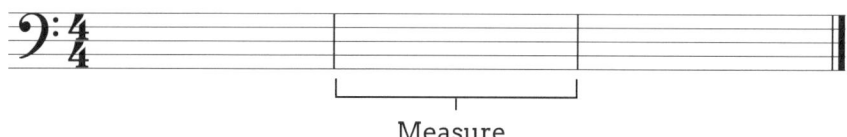

Measure

Bass Clef
Also known as the F clef.

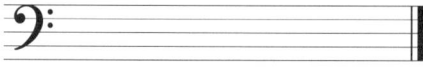

Bass Clef

Final Bar Line
Shows the end of the music.

Final Bar Line

Time Signature
The top number refers to the number of counts or beats in a measure. The bottom number informs you what length of note receives one beat.

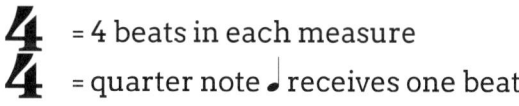

= 4 beats in each measure
= quarter note ♩ receives one beat

Bass Clef
Time Signature
Measure

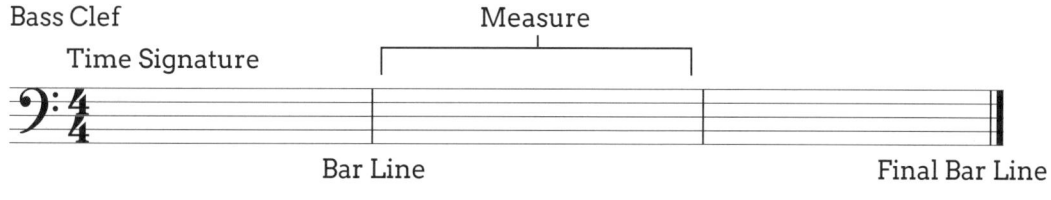

Bar Line
Final Bar Line

♭ **FLAT**
Lowers a note one half step

♯ **SHARP**
Raises a note one half step

LESSON 4:
Long Tones

Begin each long tone exercise by taking a big breath for four counts. When taking a breath, the throat should be open, much like yawning. In addition, allow space to be present between the top and bottom teeth. Keep the shoulders relaxed and focus on the chest cavity expanding out while silently taking in a breath. **ALWAYS START EACH NOTE BY "TONGUING"** (*moving your tongue as if you were saying "ta"*).

The seven slide positions are shown below and in the video titled "Slide Postitions."

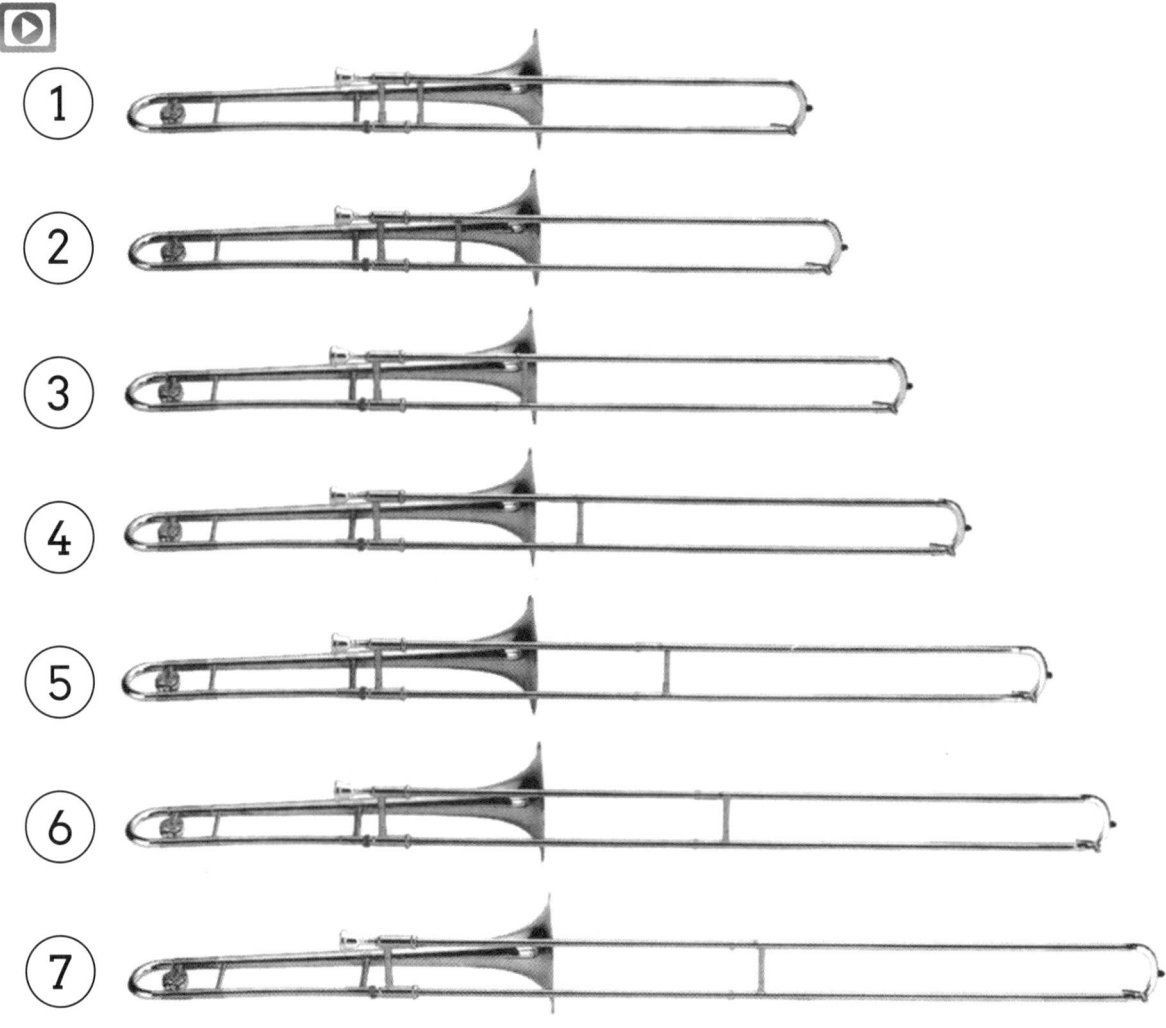

Using the slide positions shown, hold each note as long as possible. Be sure to take a four-count breath before changing slide positions. Move your slide as fast as possible to the next position.

1.

Play in each position for four counts, trying to play two measures in one breath. At the end of the second measure, exhale any remaining air for two counts, inhale for two counts and continue through the exercise.

2.

> **TOOLBOX**
>
> **'**
> A **breath mark** tells you where to breathe in a piece of music.

Play in each position for two counts. Observe where you should be breathing, taking two counts to breathe.

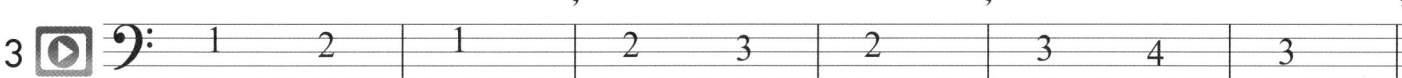

Play in each position for two counts. Observe where you should be breathing, taking two counts to breathe.

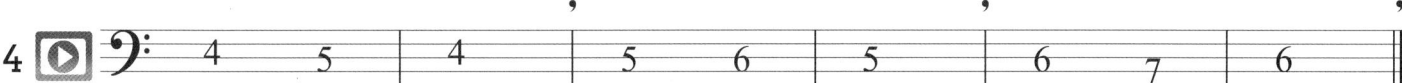

Whole Note

A **whole note** receives four counts (or beats) of sound in 4/4 time.

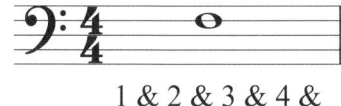

1 & 2 & 3 & 4 &

Whole Rest

A **whole rest** receives four counts (or beats) of silence in 4/4 time.

1 & 2 & 3 & 4 &

Time Signature

4 = 4 beats in each measure
4 = quarter note ♩ receives one beat

Using the slide positions shown, hold each note for four counts. Be sure to take a quick breath before changing slide positions.

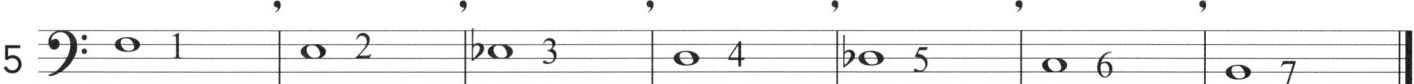

Using the slide positions shown, hold each note for four counts. Notice the rests are also four counts. When you move to a new position, move your slide as quickly as possible.

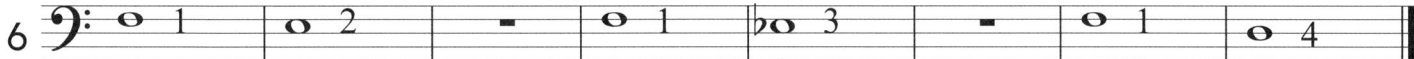

Repeat the same instructions as the previous exercise.

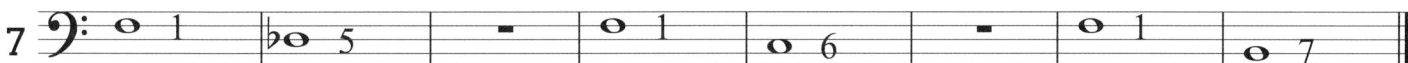

Tone Exercise. Breathe as necessary.

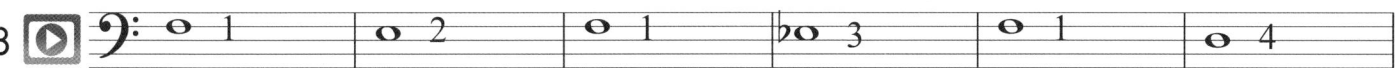

Half Note

A **half note** receives two counts (or beats) of sound in 4/4 time.

1 & 2 & 3 & 4 &

Half Rest

A **half rest** receives two counts (or beats) of silence in 4/4 time.

1 & 2 & 3 & 4 &

Using the slide positions show, hold each note for two counts. Notice the rests are also two counts.

Always start your buzz by moving your tongue as if you were saying "ta."

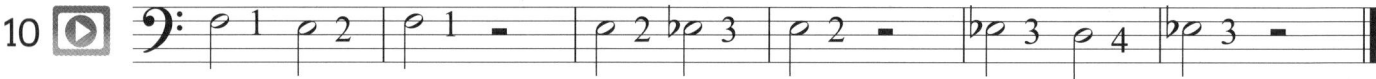

Repeat the same instructions as the previous exercise.

Tone Exercise: Part 1

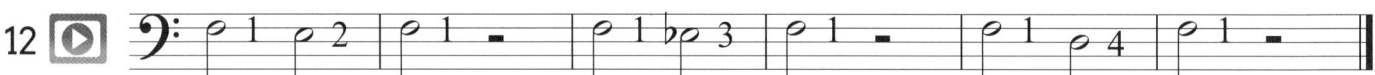

Tone Exercise: Part 2

Combine whole notes and half notes in this complete Tone Exercise.

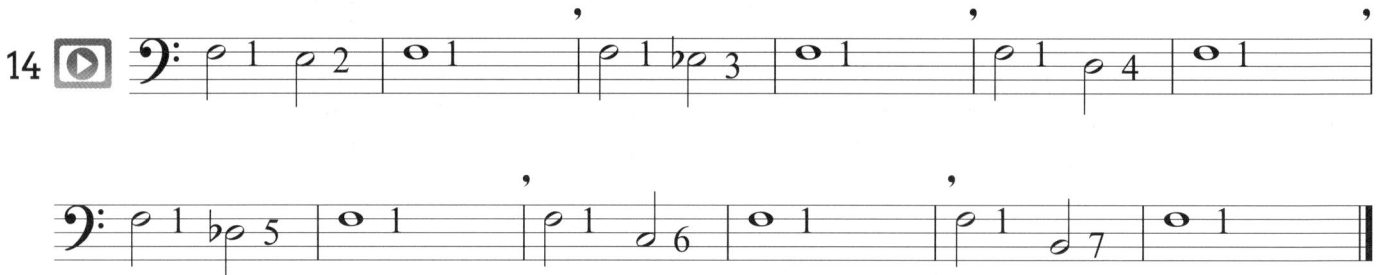

PLAYING LOWER

TOOLBOX TIP

PLAYING LOWER

You can make your trombone sound lower by relaxing your embouchure and allowing the aperture to be larger.

Think about the size of the hole between your lips if they were wrapped around a wide straw in your mouth. This is how it should feel when you are trying to produce lower sounds on your trombone.

Make your lips looser than you've been doing up to this point—let the aperture be slightly larger than the one you've been using. This will make your sound lower, even though you haven't changed slide positions!

1

Keeping your lips loose, take in a big breath and play 2 measures before your next breath. There should be no tightness in your shoulders when you breathe.

2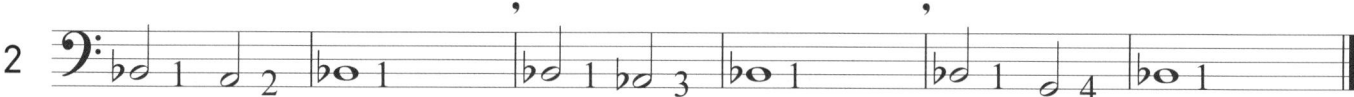

Repeat the same instructions as the previous exercise.

3

Check the first note in the measure - you begin in a different slide position!

4

Observe the breath marks. Use the rest in the middle to take a full breath before starting again.

5

LESSON 5:
Reading Notes

The Musical Alphabet uses the letters A through G. (A-B-C-D-E-F-G-A-B-C, etc.).

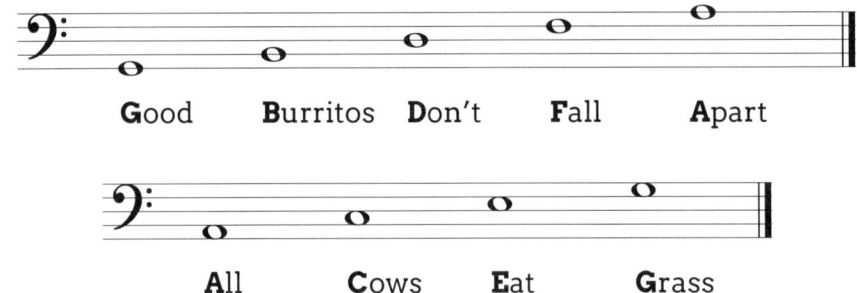

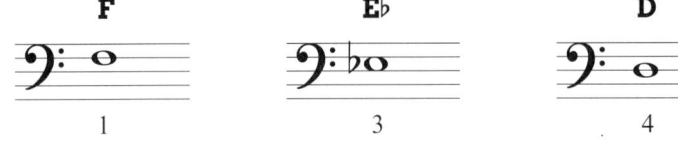

Subdivision
Breaking the beat into smaller, even pieces, rather than just counting the strong beats.
(Ex: *1 & 2 & 3 & 4 &*)

Flat ♭
Lowers the pitch of the note one half-step.

Half Step
The smallest interval in traditional music. (Changing an E to an E♭ lowers the note a half-step.)

Remember to always start each note with your tongue!

NEW NOTE: F

Count: 1 & 2 & 3 & 4 &   1 & 2 & 3 & 4 &

NEW NOTE: E♭

The flat symbol (♭) in front of a note affects the rest of that note in that measure.

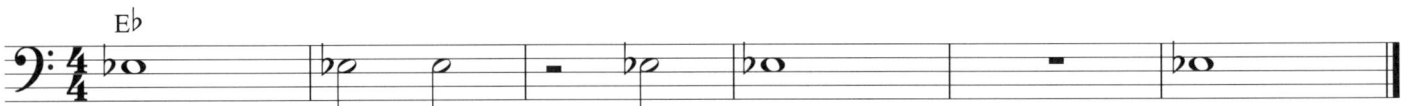

NEW NOTE: D

MIX 'EM UP

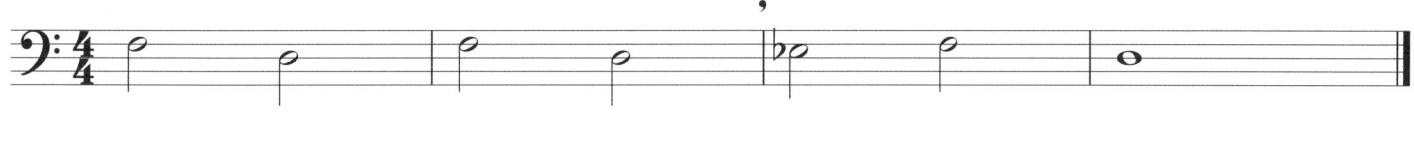

NEW NOTES: C   B♭

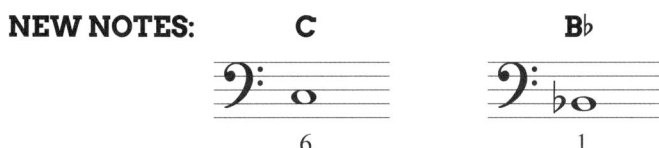

TROMBONE TALK: This B♭ is in the same position as an F, but your lips should be looser and your air should be warmer (like you are trying to steam up a window).

NEW NOTE: C

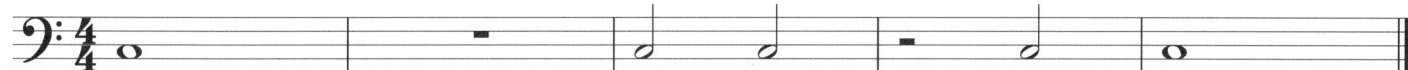

NEW NOTE: B♭

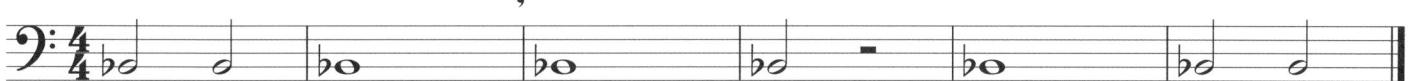

BACK 'N' FORTH

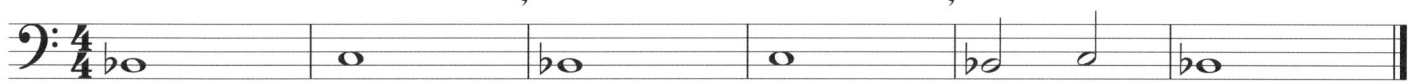

UP & DOWN

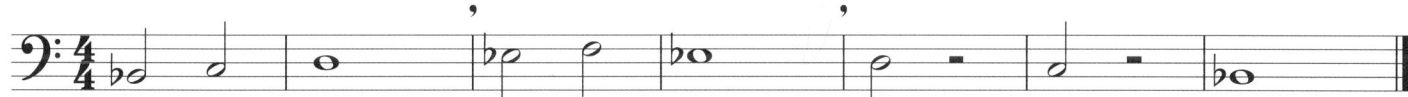

RIGHT IN THE MIDDLE

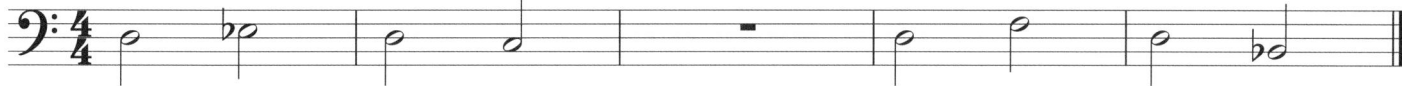

THE BELL TOWER

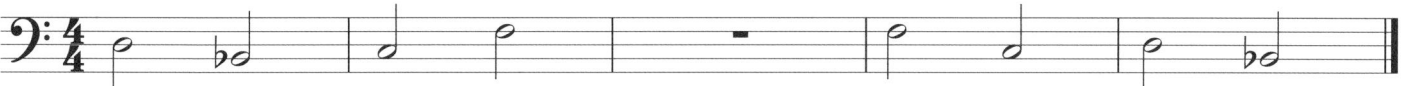

Quarter Note

1 & 2 & 3 & 4 &

A **quarter note** receives 1 count (or beat) of sound in 4/4 time.

Quarter Rest

1 & 2 & 3 & 4 &

A **quarter rest** receives 1 count (or beat) of silence in 4/4 time.

> **TOOLBOX TIP**
>
> **SLIDE SPEED**
> The slide should move as quickly as possible from one position to the next note's position. Your tongue must touch your teeth at the EXACT moment the slide arrives in the new position. Don't move your slide for the next note until the last possible second to ensure the note is held its full value.
>
> *The challenge is to make the movement occur primarily in your wrist, not your entire arm.*

RAIN, RAIN GO AWAY
Traditional

Copyright © 2022 by HAL LEONARD LLC
International Copyright Secured   All Rights Reserved

TRUMPET VOLUNTARY
By JEREMIAH CLARKE

Copyright © 2022 by HAL LEONARD LLC
International Copyright Secured   All Rights Reserved

LOVE ME TENDER
Words and Music by ELVIS PRESLEY and VERA MATSON

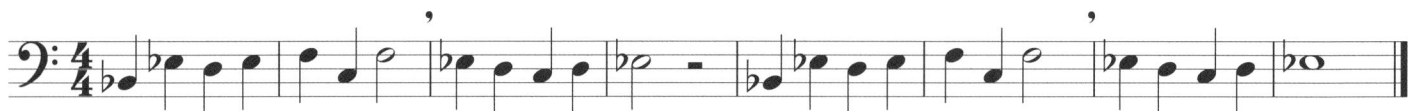

Copyright © 1956; Renewed 1984 Elvis Presley Music (BMI)
All Rights Administered by Songs Of Steve Peter and Songs Of Kobalt Music Publishing
International Copyright Secured   All Rights Reserved

MERRILY WE ROLL ALONG
Traditional

Copyright © 2022 by HAL LEONARD LLC
International Copyright Secured   All Rights Reserved

Key Signature

Indicates whether to play the note sharp, flat, or natural. Flat (♭) or sharp (♯) signs are placed after the clef. The line or space that the sharp or flat occupies indicates which notes are changed.

This key signature has 2 flats: B♭ and E♭. It is known as B♭ major.

> **TOOLBOX**
>
> **BREATHING**
>
> Breath marks do not always appear in music. If a song does not have a breath mark, breathe quickly when you need more oxygen.

ODE TO JOY
from SYMPHONY NO. 9 IN D MINOR, FOURTH MOVEMENT CHORAL THEME
Music by LUDWIG VAN BEETHOVEN

Copyright © 2022 by HAL LEONARD LLC
International Copyright Secured   All Rights Reserved

JINGLE BELLS
Words and Music by J. PIERPONT

Copyright © 2022 by HAL LEONARD LLC
International Copyright Secured   All Rights Reserved

New Key Signature: Key of E♭

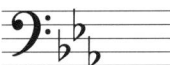

Note that there are three flats in this key signature. In this key you will play B♭, E♭, and A♭ if those notes are written in this song.

NEW NOTE: G

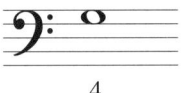

4

MY HEART WILL GO ON
(LOVE THEME FROM 'TITANIC')
from the Paramount and Twentieth Century Fox Motion Picture TITANIC
Music by JAMES HORNER • Lyric by WILL JENNINGS

Copyright © 1997 Sony Harmony, Sony Melody, T C F Music Publishing, Inc., Fox Film Music Corporation and Blue Sky Rider Songs
All Rights on behalf of Sony Harmony and Sony Melody Administered by Sony Music Publishing LLC, 424 Church Street, Suite 1200, Nashville, TN 37219
All Rights on behalf of Blue Sky Rider Songs Administered by Irving Music, Inc.
International Copyright Secured   All Rights Reserved

LONDON BRIDGE
Traditional

Copyright © 2022 by HAL LEONARD LLC
International Copyright Secured   All Rights Reserved

NOBODY KNOWS THE TROUBLE I'VE SEEN
African-American Spiritual

Copyright © 2022 by HAL LEONARD LLC
International Copyright Secured   All Rights Reserved

THE LONGEST TIME
Words and Music by BILLY JOEL

Copyright © 1983 JOELSONGS
All Rights Administered by ALMO MUSIC CORP.
All Rights Reserved   Used by Permission

Time Signature

2/4 = 2 beats in each measure
= quarter note ♩ receives one beat

Eighth Note

Count: 1 & 2 &

An **eighth note** receives 1/2 of a beat of sound. Often, they are paired in groups of two notes.

TOOLBOX TIP

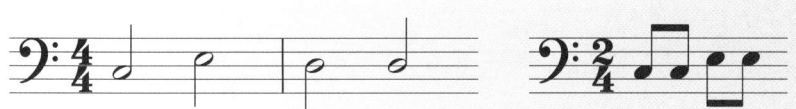

Notes can have the stem facing up or down, depending upon where they are placed in each measure. Notes above the middle line have the stems facing down, while notes below the middle line have stems facing up. Notes on the middle line can be written with the stems up or down.

BOIL THEM CABBAGE DOWN
American Folksong

Copyright © 2022 by HAL LEONARD LLC
International Copyright Secured   All Rights Reserved

FRÈRE JACQUES (ARE YOU SLEEPING?)
Traditional

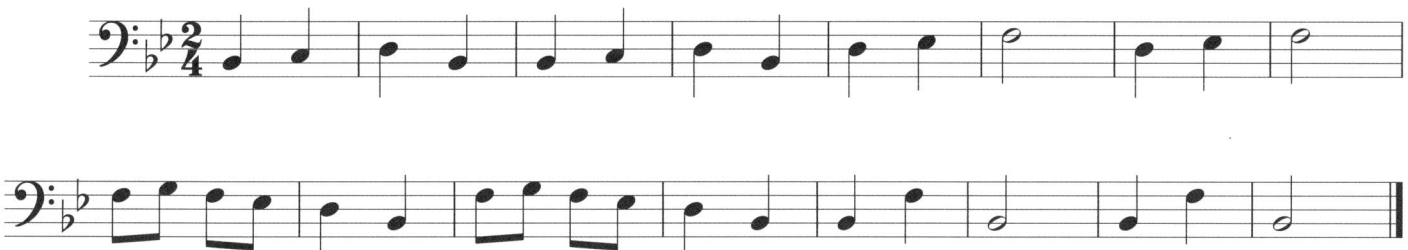

Copyright © 2022 by HAL LEONARD LLC
International Copyright Secured   All Rights Reserved

LOVE STORY
Words and Music by TAYLOR SWIFT

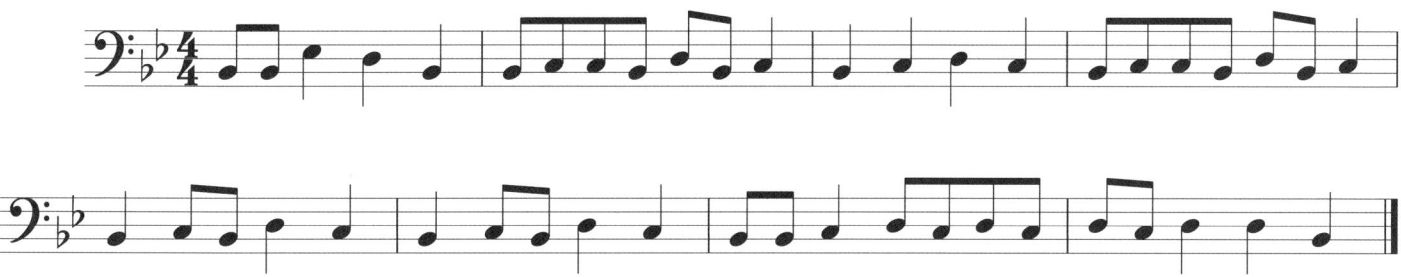

Copyright © 2008 SONGS OF UNIVERSAL, INC., TAYLOR SWIFT MUSIC and SONY MUSIC PUBLISHING (US) LLC
All Rights for TAYLOR SWIFT MUSIC Administered by SONGS OF UNIVERSAL, INC.
All Rights for SONY MUSIC PUBLISHING (US) LLC Administered by SONY MUSIC PUBLISHING (US) LLC, 424 Church Street, Suite 1200, Nashville, TN 37219
All Rights Reserved   Used by Permission

Dynamics

Indicate how loud or soft to play the music.

f **Forte:** Loud p **Piano:** Soft

Repeat Sign

Instructs you to go back to the beginning of the piece of music.

THE SIAMESE CAT SONG
from LADY AND THE TRAMP
Words and Music by SONNY BURKE and PEGGY LEE

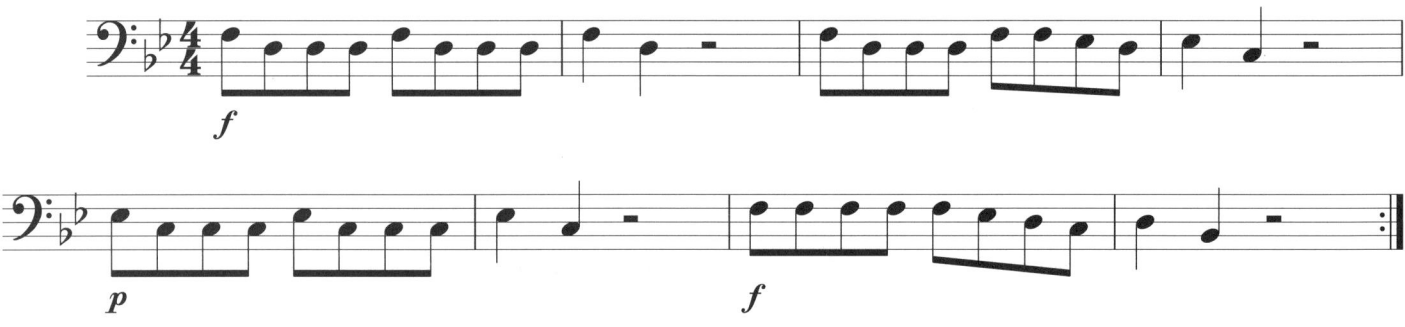

© 1953 Walt Disney Music Company
Copyright Renewed.
All Rights Reserved. Used by Permission.

I LOVE ROCK 'N ROLL
Words and Music by ALAN MERRILL and JAKE HOOKER

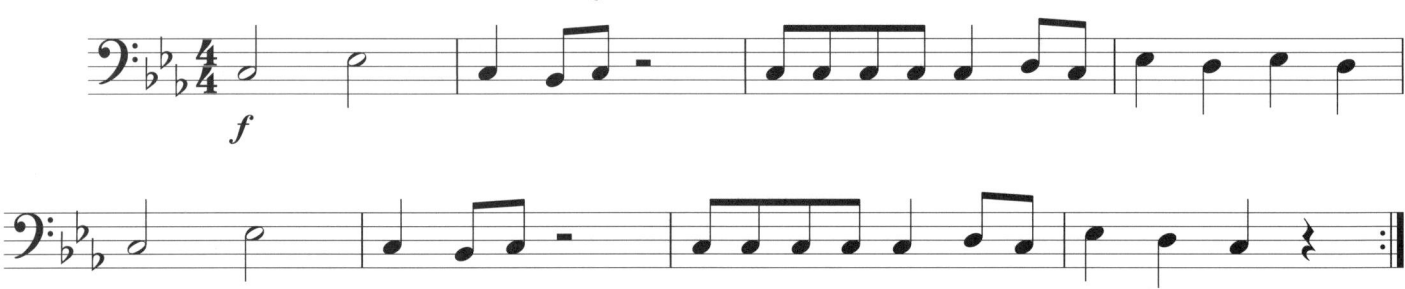

Copyright © 1975, 1982 Finchley Music Corp. and RAK Publishing Ltd.
Copyright Renewed
All Rights for the U.S. and Canada Administered by Kobalt Songs Music Publishing
International Copyright Secured   All Rights Reserved

WE ARE FAMILY
Words and Music by NILE RODGERS and BERNARD EDWARDS

Copyright © 1979 Sony Music Publishing LLC and Bernard's Other Music
All Rights on behalf of Sony Music Publishing LLC Administered by Sony Music Publishing LLC, 424 Church Street, Suite 1200, Nashville, TN 37219
All Rights on behalf of Bernard's Other Music Administered by Warner-Tamerlane Publishing Corp.
International Copyright Secured   All Rights Reserved

SHEPHERD'S HEY
English Folk Song

Copyright © 2022 by HAL LEONARD LLC
International Copyright Secured   All Rights Reserved

EVERY BREATH YOU TAKE
Music and Lyrics by STING

Copyright © 1983 G.M. Sumner
All Rights Administered by Sony Music Publishing LLC, 424 Church Street, Suite 1200, Nashville, TN 37219
International Copyright Secured   All Rights Reserved

> **TROMBONE TALK: TUNING**
>
> The trombone has a tuning slide that can be adjusted if the instrument is sharp or flat. Using a tuner or a tuner app, play an F and note if you are out of tune. If your instrument is sharp, you need to make your instrument slightly longer by pulling out the tuning slide. If you are flat, your tuning slide should be pushed in to make the instrument just a little shorter. **SHARP – OUT, FLAT – IN**
>
> *These concepts can also be applied to each slide position for tuning individual notes.*

THE VICTORS (MICHIGAN FIGHT SONG)
By LOUIS ELBEL

© 1928 (Renewed) EDWIN H. MORRIS & COMPANY, A Division of MPL Music Publishing, Inc.
All Rights Reserved

Dynamics

mf Mezzo Forte: Medium Loud

mp Mezzo Piano: Medium Soft

Double Bar

Indicates a new section within the music.

PART OF YOUR WORLD
from THE LITTLE MERMAID
Music by ALAN MENKEN • Lyrics by HOWARD ASHMAN

© 1988 Wonderland Music Company, Inc. and Walt Disney Music Company
All Rights Reserved. Used by Permission.

Time Signature

3/4 = 3 beats in each measure
= quarter note ♩ receives one beat

Tie

Connects two or more notes of the same pitch to make one longer note.

This note is now held for two beats.

MORNING
from PEER GYNT
By EDVARD GRIEG

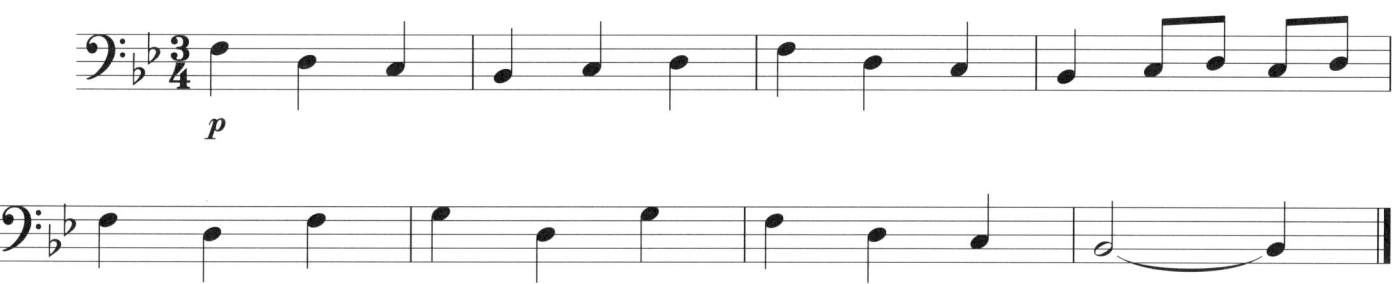

Copyright © 2022 by HAL LEONARD LLC
International Copyright Secured   All Rights Reserved

ALLEGRO ("SPRING")
from CONCERTO IN E MAJOR "SPRING," OP. 8, NO. 1
By Antonio Vivaldi

Copyright © 2022 by HAL LEONARD LLC
International Copyright Secured   All Rights Reserved

Dotted Half Note

A **dotted half note** receives three counts (or beats) of sound.

> **TOOLBOX**
> A dot adds half of the value of the note. If a half note is worth 2 beats, the dot would would add half of the value to the existing note. (2 + 1 = 3 beats.)

PIANO MAN
Words and Music by BILLY JOEL

Copyright © 1973 JOELSONGS
Copyright Renewed
All Rights Administered by ALMO MUSIC CORP.
All Rights Reserved   Used by Permission

HALLELUJAH CHORUS
By GEORGE FRIDERIC HANDEL

Copyright © 2022 by HAL LEONARD LLC
International Copyright Secured   All Rights Reserved

BLOWIN' IN THE WIND
Words and Music by BOB DYLAN

Copyright © 1962 UNIVERSAL TUNES
Copyright Renewed
All Rights Reserved   Used by Permission

TRUE COLORS
Words and Music by BILLY STEINBERG and TOM KELLY

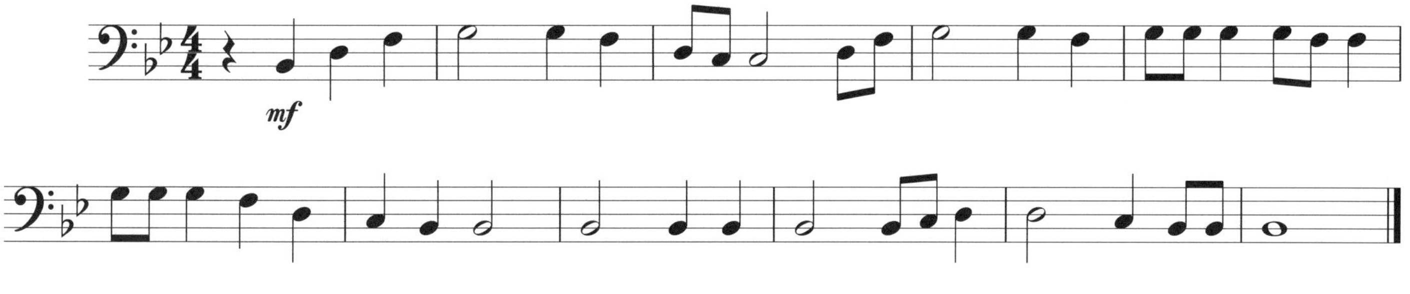

Copyright © 1986 Sony Music Publishing LLC
All Rights Administered by Sony Music Publishing LLC, 424 Church Street, Suite 1200, Nashville, TN 37219
International Copyright Secured   All Rights Reserved

Tempo
The speed of the music.

Moderato: Medium tempo

Intonation
Pitch accuracy

To play with good **intonation** means you have the ability to play your instrument in tune.

> **TROMBONE TALK**
> Playing the trombone can seem challenging because there are no clearly marked positions aside from first position. Even professional trombone players have to constantly make small adjustments to the slide positions to make the notes sound correct with good intonation.

THE MEDALLION CALLS
from PIRATES OF THE CARIBBEAN: THE CURSE OF THE BLACK PEARL
Music by KLAUS BADELT

© 2003 Walt Disney Music Company
All Rights Reserved. Used by Permission.

More Tempos

Allegro: Fast tempo
Andante: Slower "walking" tempo (slower than Moderato)

NEW NOTE: A

LEAN ON ME
Words and Music by BILL WITHERS

Copyright © 1972 INTERIOR MUSIC CORP.
Copyright Renewed
All Rights Controlled and Administered by SONGS OF UNIVERSAL, INC.
All Rights Reserved   Used by Permission

THEME FROM "JAWS"
from the Universal Picture JAWS
By JOHN WILLIAMS

Copyright © 1975 USI B MUSIC PUBLISHING
Copyright Renewed
All Rights Controlled and Administered by SONGS OF UNIVERSAL, INC.
All Rights Reserved   Used by Permission

1st and 2nd Endings

Play through the first ending and repeat back. Once you have repeated the first time, skip the first ending and continue to the second ending.

CHIAPANECAS
Mexican Folk Song

Copyright © 2022 by HAL LEONARD LLC
International Copyright Secured   All Rights Reserved

TOOLBOX TIP

INTERNAL REPEATS

Not all repeats send you back to the beginning of a song. If you find a repeat sign at the beginning of a measure, that is where you return on the repeat.

NEW NOTE: A♭

BAD ROMANCE
Words and Music by Stefani Germanotta and Nadir Khayat

Copyright © 2009 Sony Music Publishing LLC and House Of Gaga Publishing Inc.
All Rights Administered by Sony Music Publishing LLC, 424 Church Street, Suite 1200, Nashville, TN 37219
International Copyright Secured   All Rights Reserved

OPEN ARMS
Words and Music by STEVE PERRY and JONATHAN CAIN

Copyright © 1981 Lacey Boulevard Music (BMI) and Weed-High Nightmare Music (BMI)
All Rights for Weed-High Nightmare Music Administered by Wixen Music Publishing Inc.
International Copyright Secured   All Rights Reserved

Pickup Note

A note or group of notes that occur before the first full measure of music.

> **TOOLBOX TIP**
>
> If the music has a pickup note or notes, the beats that were used in the pickup measure are often taken from the last measure of music.
>
>
>
> **IF** one beat is moved to the beginning as a pickup meaure
>
> **THEN** one beat is taken from the last measure.

WILLIAM TELL OVERTURE
By GIOACHINO ROSSINI

Copyright © 2022 by HAL LEONARD LLC
International Copyright Secured   All Rights Reserved

SECRETS
Words and Music by RYAN TEDDER

Copyright © 2009 Sony Music Publishing LLC, Velvet Hammer Music and Midnite Miracle Music
All Rights Administered by Sony Music Publishing LLC, 424 Church Street, Suite 1200, Nashville, TN 37219
International Copyright Secured   All Rights Reserved

I JUST CAN'T WAIT TO BE KING
from THE LION KING

Music by ELTON JOHN • Lyrics by TIM RICE

© 1994 Wonderland Music Company, Inc.
All Rights Reserved. Used by Permission.

TOOLBOX TIP

METRONOME
A **metronome** is a device used to keep a steady tempo.

Setting a metronome to the tempo of the piece of music being practiced is key to developing good musicianship. Unless otherwise marked, music is intended to be played at the same speed throughout the piece. When a passage of music is challenging or becoming difficult, slow down the metronome to practice the notes and rhythms correctly. Once mastery of the concept at a slower tempo has been achieved, gradually increase the tempo and continue to practice until the original tempo is reached.

CARNIVAL OF VENICE
By JULIUS BENEDICT

Copyright © 2022 by HAL LEONARD LLC
International Copyright Secured   All Rights Reserved

Dotted Quarter Note

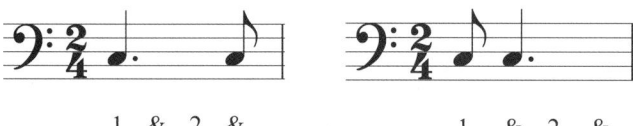

A **dotted quarter note** is worth 1-1/2 beats. The dot adds half of the value of the note to the existing note. (1 + 1/2 = 1-1/2) Dotted quarter notes are often accompanied by a single eighth note.

TOOLBOX

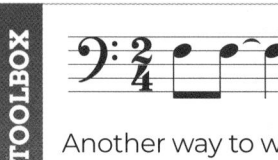

Another way to write a note is that is 1-1/2 beats is to tie an eighth note to a quarter note.

New Tempo
Largo: Very slow

LARGO
from SYMPHONY NO. 9 IN E MINOR, OP. 95 ("From THE NEW WORLD")
By ANTONÍN DVOŘÁK

Copyright © 2022 by HAL LEONARD LLC
International Copyright Secured All Rights Reserved

MY GIRL
Words and Music by SMOKEY ROBINSON and RONALD WHITE

Copyright © 1964 Jobete Music Co., Inc. and Bourne Co. (ASCAP)
Copyright Renewed
All Rights on behalf of Jobete Music Co., Inc. Administered by Sony Music Publishing LLC, 424 Church Street, Suite 1200, Nashville, TN 37219
International Copyright Secured All Rights Reserved

TOOLBOX

SHUFFLE
A rhythmic feel where the first note in a group of two eighth notes feels twice as long than the second note. This groove is often found in pop music.

The shuffle feel is also used in many jazz pieces of music which will be explored later in this book.

MICKEY MOUSE MARCH
from THE MICKEY MOUSE CLUB
Words and Music by JIMMIE DODD

© 1955 Walt Disney Music Company
Copyright Renewed.
All Rights Reserved. Used by Permission.

ISN'T SHE LOVELY
Words and Music by STEVIE WONDER

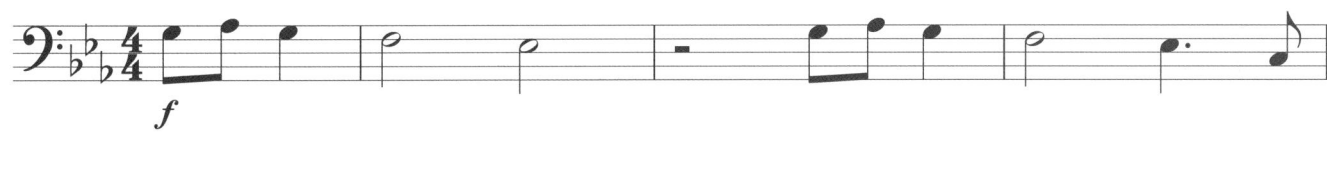

Copyright © 1976 Jobete Music Co., Inc. and Black Bull Music
Copyright Renewed
All Rights Administered by Sony Music Publishing LLC, 424 Church Street, Suite 1200, Nashville, TN 37219
International Copyright Secured   All Rights Reserved

ROSANNA
Words and Music by DAVID PAICH

Copyright © 1982 Hudmar Publishing Co., Inc.
All Rights Controlled and Administered by Spirit Two Music, Inc.
International Copyright Secured   All Rights Reserved

EIGHT DAYS A WEEK
Words and Music by JOHN LENNON and PAUL McCARTNEY

Copyright © 1964 Sony Music Publishing LLC and MPL Communications, Inc. in the United States
Copyright Renewed
All Rights for the world excluding the United States Administered by Sony Music Publishing LLC, 424 Church Street, Suite 1200, Nashville, TN 37219
International Copyright Secured   All Rights Reserved

TOOLBOX

INTERVAL
The distance between notes.

Octave
An interval between two notes that have the same note name. Octaves are eight notes apart.

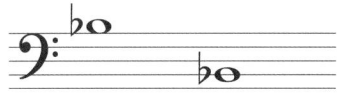

NEW NOTE:

A
2

B♭
1

TOOLBOX You have already learned the lower version of these two notes. To make your sound higher, use the same technique as you did when doing buzzing exercises: tighten your lips and buzz FAST air. Aiming your airstream down may also help!

B♭ MAJOR SCALE

The first eight notes of *Joy to the World* are a descending scale.

JOY TO THE WORLD
Music by GEORGE FRIDERIC HANDEL · Adapted by LOWELL MASON

Copyright © 2022 by HAL LEONARD LLC
International Copyright Secured   All Rights Reserved

MR. TAMBOURINE MAN
Words and Music by BOB DYLAN

Copyright © 1964, 1965 UNIVERSAL TUNES
Copyright Renewed
All Rights Reserved   Used by Permission

ALL MY LOVING
Words and Music by JOHN LENNON and PAUL McCARTNEY

Copyright © 1963, 1964 Sony Music Publishing LLC and MPL Communications, Inc. in the United States
Copyright Renewed
All Rights for the world excluding the United States Administered by Sony Music Publishing LLC, 424 Church Street, Suite 1200, Nashville, TN 37219
International Copyright Secured   All Rights Reserved

INTO THE UNKNOWN
from FROZEN 2
Music and Lyrics by KRISTEN ANDERSON-LOPEZ and ROBERT LOPEZ

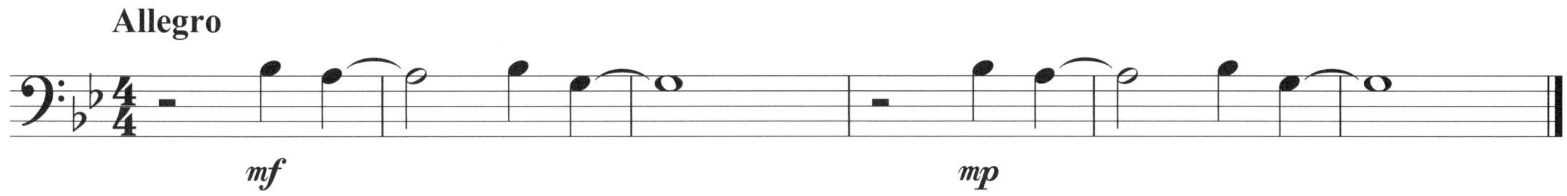

© 2019 Wonderland Music Company, Inc.
All Rights Reserved. Used by Permission.

CAN YOU FEEL THE LOVE TONIGHT
from THE LION KING
Music by ELTON JOHN • Lyrics by TIM RICE

© 1994 Wonderland Music Company, Inc.
All Rights Reserved. Used by Permission.

FIREWORK

Words and Music by KATY PERRY, MIKKEL ERIKSEN,
TOR ERIK HERMANSEN, ESTHER DEAN and SANDY WILHELM

© 2010 WHEN I'M RICH YOU'LL BE MY BITCH, EMI MUSIC PUBLISHING LTD., PEERMUSIC III, LTD., DAT DAMN DEAN MUSIC, 2412 LLC, DIPIU SRL and ULTRA INTERNATIONAL MUSIC PUBLISHING LLC
All Rights for WHEN I'M RICH YOU'LL BE MY BITCH Administered by WC MUSIC CORP.
All Rights for EMI MUSIC PUBLISHING LTD. Administered by SONY MUSIC PUBLISHING LLC, 424 Church Street, Suite 1200, Nashville, TN 37219
All Rights for DAT DAMN DEAN MUSIC and 2412 LLC Controlled and Administered by PEERMUSIC III, LTD.
All Rights for DIPIU SRL Administered by DOWNTOWN DMP SONGS
All Rights for ULTRA INTERNATIONAL MUSIC PUBLISHING LLC in the U.S. and Canada Administered by ULTRA TUNES
All Rights Reserved   Used by Permission

FIELDS OF GOLD
Music and Lyrics by STING

Copyright © 1993 Steerpike Ltd.
All Rights Administered by Sony Music Publishing LLC, 424 Church Street, Suite 1200, Nashville, TN 37219
International Copyright Secured   All Rights Reserved

New Key Signature: Key of A♭

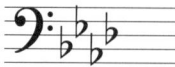

Note that there are four flats in this key signature. In this key you will play B♭, E♭, A♭ and D♭.

NEW NOTE:

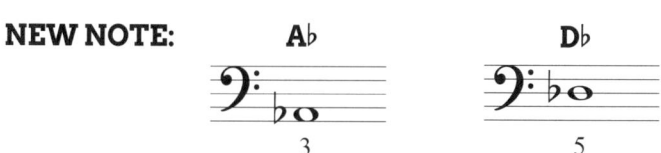

A♭ MAJOR SCALE

ON TOP OF OLD SMOKEY
Kentucky Mountain Folksong

ARIRANG
Korean Folksong

MOON RIVER
from the Paramount Picture BREAKFAST AT TIFFANY'S
Words by JOHNNY MERCER • Music by HENRY MANCINI

Moderato

Copyright © 1961 Sony Music Publishing LLC
Copyright Renewed
All Rights Administered by Sony Music Publishing LLC, 424 Church Street, Suite 1200, Nashville, TN 37219
International Copyright Secured   All Rights Reserved

SHE DRIVES ME CRAZY
Words and Music by DAVID STEELE and ROLAND GIFT

Moderato

Copyright © 1988 UNIVERSAL MUSIC PUBLISHING LTD.
All Rights Administered by UNIVERSAL - POLYGRAM INTERNATIONAL PUBLISHING, INC.
All Rights Reserved   Used by Permission

43

FORREST GUMP – MAIN TITLE (FEATHER THEME)

from the Paramount Motion Picture FORREST GUMP

Music by ALAN SILVESTRI

Copyright © 1994 Sony Music Publishing LLC
All Rights Administered by Sony Music Publishing LLC, 424 Church Street, Suite 1200, Nashville, TN 37219
International Copyright Secured   All Rights Reserved

I'M A BELIEVER

Words and Music by NEIL DIAMOND

Copyright © 1966 TALLYRAND MUSIC, INC. and EMI FORAY MUSIC
Copyright Renewed
All Rights for TALLYRAND MUSIC, INC. Administered by UNIVERSAL TUNES
All Rights for EMI FORAY MUSIC Administered by SONY MUSIC PUBLISHING LLC, 424 Church Street, Suite 1200, Nashville, TN 37219
All Rights Reserved   Used by Permission

TOOLBOX TIPS

TEMPO MARKINGS

Tempos are measured in bpm, or beats per minute. When setting your metronome, consider these speeds for each tempo:

Allegro: 120-160 bpm **Andante:** 80-100 bpm **Largo:** 40-60 bpm
Moderato: 100-120 bpm **Adagio:** 60-80 bpm

MY FAVORITE THINGS
from THE SOUND OF MUSIC
Lyrics by OSCAR HAMMERSTEIN II • Music by RICHARD RODGERS

Copyright © 1959 Williamson Music Company c/o Concord Music Publishing
Copyright Renewed
All Rights Reserved Used by Permission

Natural ♮

A **natural sign** cancels all previous accidentals or sharps and flats in a key signature for the duration of that measure. It is often referred to as returning a note back to its **normal**, or natural state.

These two notes are the same, however one is written with a natural sign because of the key signature.

> **TOOLBOX TIPS**
>
> **ACCIDENTALS**
>
> An **accidental** is a sharp, flat or natural that appears in a measure. The note stays altered for the entire measure or until another accidental changes that pitch.
>
> A courtesy accidental is a reminder that a note already exists in the key signature. It is sometimes placed in parentheses. (♮)

AQUARIUS
from HAIR
Words by JAMES RADO and GEROME RAGNI • Music by GALT MacDERMOT

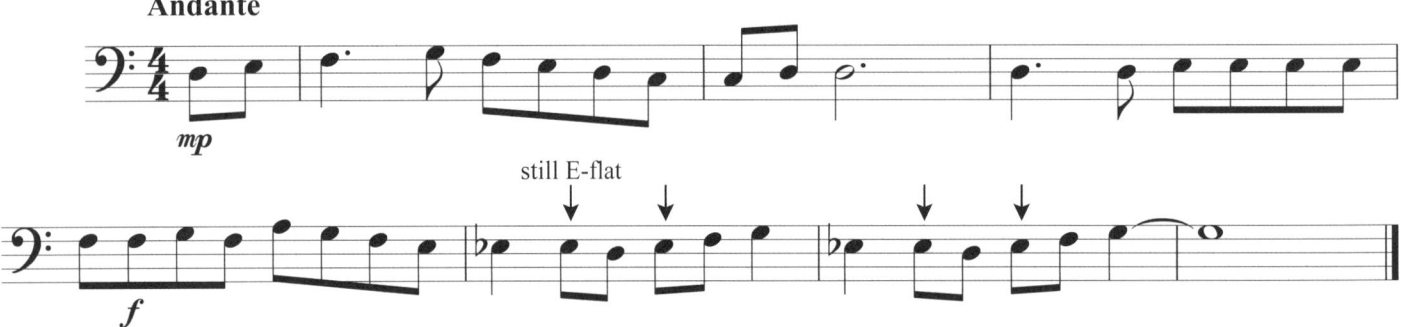

© 1966, 1967, 1968, 1970 (Renewed) JAMES RADO, GEROME RAGNI, GALT MacDERMOT, NAT SHAPIRO and EMI U CATALOG INC.
All Rights Administered by EMI U CATALOG INC. (Publishing) and ALFRED MUSIC (Print)
All Rights Reserved   Used by Permission

New Tempo
Adagio: Slow

JUPITER
from THE PLANETS
By GUSTAV HOLST

Copyright © 2022 by HAL LEONARD LLC
International Copyright Secured   All Rights Reserved

(SITTIN' ON) THE DOCK OF THE BAY
Words and Music by STEVE CROPPER and OTIS REDDING

Copyright © 1968 IRVING MUSIC, INC.
Copyright Renewed
All Rights Reserved   Used by Permission

25 OR 6 TO 4
Words and Music by ROBERT LAMM

Copyright © 1970 Lamminations Music and Spirit Catalog Holdings, S.a.r.l.
Copyright Renewed
All Rights for Lamminations Music Administered by BMG Rights Management (US) LLC
All Rights for Spirit Catalog Holdings, S.a.r.l. Controlled and Administered by Spirit Two Music, Inc.
International Copyright Secured   All Rights Reserved

THEME FROM "JURASSIC PARK"
from the Universal Motion Picture JURASSIC PARK
Composed by JOHN WILLIAMS

Copyright © 1993 USI B MUSIC PUBLISHING
All Rights Controlled and Administered by SONGS OF UNIVERSAL, INC.
All Rights Reserved   Used by Permission

MANEATER
Words and Music by SARA ALLEN, DARYL HALL and JOHN OATES

Copyright © 1982 Geomantic Music, Hot Cha Music Co. and Unichappell Music, Inc.
All Rights for Geomantic Music and Hot Cha Music Co. Administered by BMG Rights Management (US) LLC
All Rights Reserved   Used by Permission

WE FOUND LOVE
Words and Music by CALVIN HARRIS

Copyright © 2011 EMI Music Publishing Ltd.
All Rights Administered by Sony Music Publishing LLC, 424 Church Street, Suite 1200, Nashville, TN 37219
International Copyright Secured   All Rights Reserved

LESSON 6:
Syncopation

Eighth Rest

An **eighth rest** receives 1/2 of a beat of silence.

Syncopation

When the feeling shifts from the strong beat to the offbeat, this rhythmic change is called **syncopation**.

Offbeats

An **offbeat** is a beat that is not on the strong beat, or a "number" in a measure. Offbeats fall in between the beat in which you would tap your foot. When counting, this is generally the word "and."

MINUET IN G MAJOR
from NOTEBOOK FOR ANNA MAGDALENA BACH
By CHRISTIAN PETZOLD

Copyright © 2022 by HAL LEONARD LLC
International Copyright Secured   All Rights Reserved

LEAN ON ME
Words and Music by BILL WITHERS

Copyright © 1972 INTERIOR MUSIC CORP.
Copyright Renewed
All Rights Controlled and Administered by SONGS OF UNIVERSAL, INC.
All Rights Reserved   Used by Permission

YOU ARE THE SUNSHINE OF MY LIFE
Words and Music by STEVIE WONDER

Copyright © 1972 Jobete Music Co., Inc. and Black Bull Music
Copyright Renewed
All Rights Administered by Sony Music Publishing LLC, 424 Church Street, Suite 1200, Nashville, TN 37219
International Copyright Secured   All Rights Reserved

NOWHERE MAN
Words and Music by JOHN LENNON and PAUL McCARTNEY

Copyright © 1965 Sony Music Publishing LLC
Copyright Renewed
All Rights Administered by Sony Music Publishing LLC, 424 Church Street, Suite 1200, Nashville, TN 37219
International Copyright Secured   All Rights Reserved

FIREFLIES
Words and Music by ADAM YOUNG

Copyright © 2009 UNIVERSAL MUSIC CORP. and OCEAN CITY PARK
All Rights Controlled and Administered by UNIVERSAL MUSIC CORP.
All Rights Reserved   Used by Permission

BLISTER IN THE SUN
Words and Music by GORDON GANO

Copyright © 1983 Gorno Music
All Rights Administered Worldwide by Kobalt Songs Music Publishing
All Rights Reserved   Used by Permission

BAD, BAD LEROY BROWN

Words and Music by JIM CROCE

HEY, SOUL SISTER

Words and Music by PAT MONAHAN, ESPEN LIND and AMUND BJORKLUND

Copyright © 2009 EMI April Music Inc., Blue Lamp Music and Stellar Songs Ltd.
All Rights Administered by Sony Music Publishing LLC, 424 Church Street, Suite 1200, Nashville, TN 37219
International Copyright Secured All Rights Reserved

TAKE ON ME

Music by PAL WAAKTAAR and MAGNE FURUHOLMNE
Words by PAL WAAKTAAR, MAGNE FURUHOLMNE and MORTEN HARKET

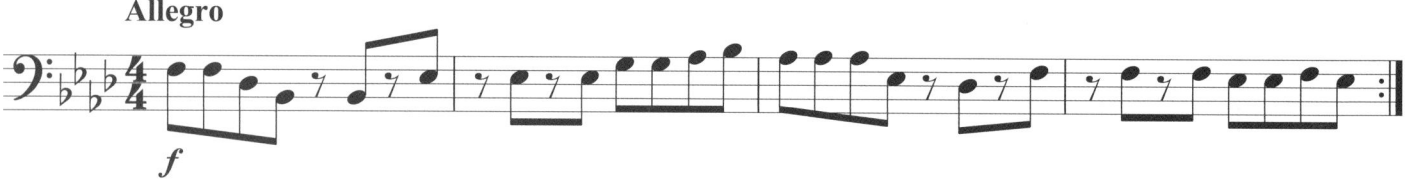

Copyright © 1984, 1985 Sony Music Publishing LLC
All Rights Administered by Sony Music Publishing LLC, 424 Church Street, Suite 1200, Nashville, TN 37219
International Copyright Secured   All Rights Reserved

On *Yeah!*, notice the first and second half sound the same because two eighth notes tied together are the same length as one quarter note.

YEAH!

Words and Music by JAMES PHILLIPS, LA MARQUIS JEFFERSON,
CHRISTOPHER BRIDGES, JONATHAN SMITH and SEAN GARRETT

Copyright © 2004 EMI April Music Inc., Ludacris Music Publishing Inc., Air Control Music, Basajamba Music, Me And Marq Music, Christopher Garrett's Publishing, Hitco South, Christopher Matthew Music, Hitco Music and Reservoir 416
All Rights on behalf of EMI April Music Inc., Ludacris Music Publishing Inc., Air Control Music and Basajamba Music Administered by Sony Music Publishing LLC, 424 Church Street, Suite 1200, Nashville, TN 37219
All Rights on behalf of Me And Marq Music, Christopher Garrett's Publishing, Hitco South, Christopher Matthew Music and Hitco Music Administered by BMG Rights Management (US) LLC
All Rights on behalf of Reservoir 416 Administered by Reservoir Media Management, Inc.
International Copyright Secured   All Rights Reserved

> **TOOLBOX TIPS**
>
> **POP MUSIC – AABA FORM**
>
> Many pieces from the Broadway and popular music idioms are comprised of two melodic ideas, labeled A and B. Often these ideas are 8 measures in length. The A "theme" is repeated twice, followed by the B "theme," often referred to as the **bridge**, as it connects the melodic ideas together. The A "theme" is restated a third time to complete the melodic material, making the form of the piece of music **AABA.**
>
> The restatement of the A theme is sometimes slightly altered (A^1), which may result in the form actually being AA^1BA^1.

DON'T KOW WHY
Words and Music by JESSE HARRIS

Copyright © 2002 Sony Music Publishing LLC and Beanly Songs
All Rights Administered by Sony Music Publishing LLC, 424 Church Street, Suite 1200, Nashville, TN 37219
International Copyright Secured   All Rights Reserved

Crescendo
Gradually get louder

Decrescendo
Gradually get softer

Occasionally a decrescendo is also called a diminuendo. Sometimes they are abbreviated in the music as: *cresc.*, *decresc.*, and *dim.* rather than using the symbols.

RIGHT HERE WAITING
Words and Music by RICHARD MARX

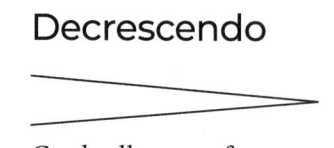

Copyright © 1989 BMG Monarch
All Rights Administered by BMG Rights Management (US) LLC
All Rights Reserved   Used by Permission

p – ***f***

Sometimes two different dynamics are shown when the music repeats. The dynamics are separated by a hyphen. Play the second dynamic on the repeat.

> **TROMBONE TALK: SLIDE ACCURACY**
> Moving from 1st to 6th position can be very challenging to execute quickly. For greater accuracy, make sure the tongue starts the new note at the exact time the slide arrives in the new position and the slide moves as fast as possible.

CAN CAN
from ORPHEUS IN THE UNDERWORLD
By Jacques Offenbach

Copyright © 2022 by HAL LEONARD LLC
International Copyright Secured   All Rights Reserved

HAPPY TOGETHER
Words and Music by GARRY BONNER and ALAN GORDON

Copyright © 1966, 1967 Trio Music Company and Alley Music Corp.
Copyright Renewed
All Rights for Trio Music Company Administered by BMG Rights Management (US) LLC
All Rights for Alley Music Corp. Administered by Round Hill Carlin, LLC
All Rights Reserved   Used by Permission

LESSON 7:
Articulations

Staccato

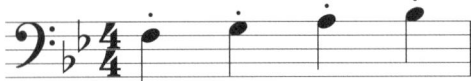

An articulation indicating that the notes are light and separated. There should be a brief silence (or separation) between the staccato notes.

> **TOOLBOX**
> **STACCATO TONGUING**
> To play **staccato**, move your tongue as if you are making the sound "TUH." *(sTUH-ccato)*
>
> There will be a slight lift between each note – keep subdividing your rhythm counting to avoid speeding up accidentally.

GHOSTBUSTERS
from the Columbia Motion Picture GHOSTBUSTERS
Words and Music by RAY PARKER, JR.

© 1984 EMI GOLDEN TORCH MUSIC CORP. and RAYDIOLA MUSIC
All Rights Reserved   Used by Permission

Quarter notes and eighth notes that are staccato will be approximately the same note length, however the amount of silence that follows the note will be different.

SUNSHINE OF YOUR LOVE
Words and Music by ERIC CLAPTON, JACK BRUCE and PETE BROWN

Copyright © 1967, 1973 E.C. Music Ltd. and Dratleaf Music, Ltd.
Copyright Renewed
International Copyright Secured   All Rights Reserved

THE MAGNIFICENT SEVEN
By ELMER BERNSTEIN

© 1960 UNITED ARTISTS MUSIC CO., INC.
Copyright Renewed by EMI U CATALOG INC.
Exclusive Print Rights Administered by ALFRED MUSIC
All Rights Reserved   Used by Permission

KARMA CHAMELEON
Words and Music by GEORGE O'DOWD, JONATHAN MOSS,
MICHAEL CRAIG, ROY HAY and PHIL PICKETT

Copyright © 1983 BMG VM Music Ltd. and Concord Entertainment Ltd.
All Rights for BMG VM Music Ltd. Administered by BMG Rights Management (US) LLC
All Rights Reserved   Used by Permission

THE BANANA BOAT SONG
Jamaican Work Song

Copyright © 2022 by HAL LEONARD LLC
International Copyright Secured   All Rights Reserved

TAINTED LOVE
Words and Music by ED COBB

Copyright © 1976 (Renewed) by Embassy Music Corporation (BMI)
International Copyright Secured   All Rights Reserved
Reprinted by Permission

THIS IS HALLOWEEN
from THE NIGHTMARE BEFORE CHRISTMAS
Music and Lyrics by DANNY ELFMAN

© 1993 Buena Vista Music Company
All Rights Reserved   Used by Permission

Allow for the silence to be present between the notes when playing staccato. Do not use your tongue to stop the end of the note. Allow the air stream to stop when playing staccato before starting the next note.

SHUT UP AND DANCE
Words and Music by RYAN McMAHON, BEN BERGER, SEAN WAUGAMAN,
ELI MAIMAN, NICHOLAS PETRICCA and KEVIN RAY

© 2014 WC MUSIC CORP., RYAN MCMAHON PUBLISHING, BENJAMIN BERGER PUBLISHING, SONY MUSIC PUBLISHING LLC, EMI APRIL MUSIC INC., ANNA SUN MUSIC, TREAT ME BETTER TINA MUSIC, VERB TO BE MUSIC and WHAT A RAUCOUS MUSIC
All Rights for RYAN MCMAHON PUBLISHING and BENJAMIN BERGER PUBLISHING Administered by WC MUSIC CORP.
All Rights for SONY MUSIC PUBLISHING LLC, EMI APRIL MUSIC INC., ANNA SUN MUSIC, TREAT ME BETTER TINA MUSIC, VERB TO BE MUSIC and WHAT A RAUCOUS MUSIC
Administered by SONY MUSIC PUBLISHING LLC, 424 Church Street, Suite 1200, Nashville, TN 37219
All Rights Reserved   Used by Permission

Accent

An articulation indicating to attack the note by playing it stronger.

 **Fortissimo:** Very loud

> **TOOLBOX**
>
> **ACCENT TONGUING**
>
> To play an **accent**, move your tongue as if you are making the sound "TEE."
>
> There should be a small amount of space between each note.

OLD TIME ROCK & ROLL
Words and Music by GEORGE JACKSON and THOMAS E. JONES III

Copyright © 1977 by Peermusic III, Ltd. and Muscle Shoals Sound Publishing
Copyright Renewed
All Rights Administered by Peermusic III, Ltd.
International Copyright Secured   All Rights Reserved

LIVIN' ON A PRAYER

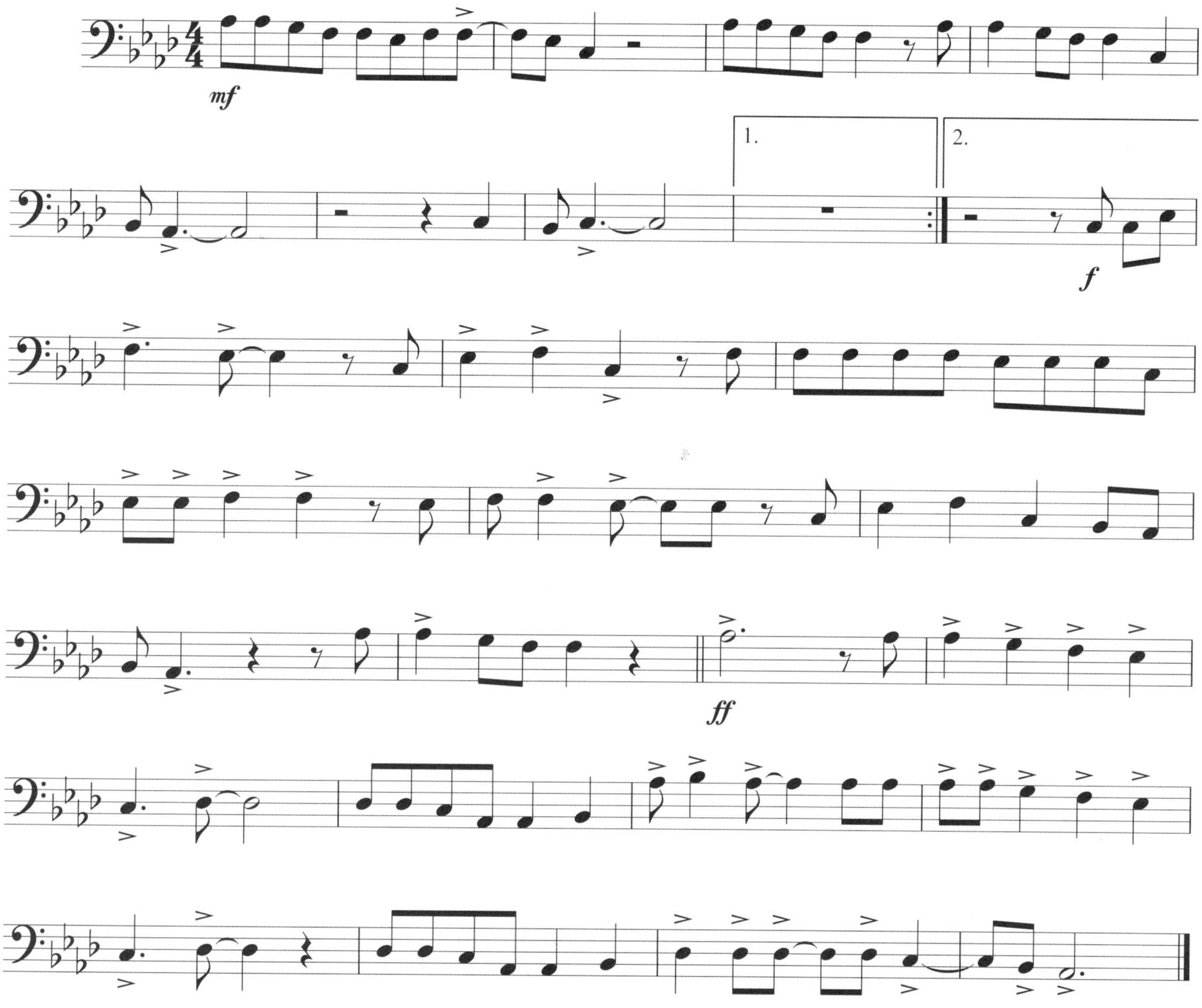

Words and Music by JON BON JOVI, DESMOND CHILD and RICHIE SAMBORA

BAD MEDICINE

Words and Music by JON BON JOVI, DESMOND CHILD and RICHIE SAMBORA

APACHE
By JERRY LORDAN

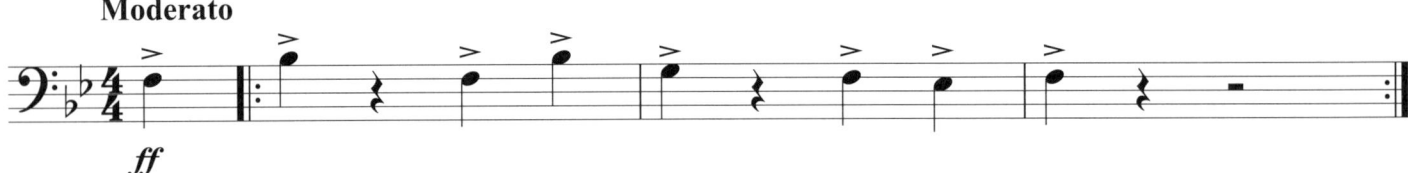

Copyright © 1960, 1961 (Renewed) by Francis, Day & Hunter Ltd., London, England
All Rights for the U.S.A. and Canada Controlled by Regent Music Corporation (BMI)
International Copyright Secured   All Rights Reserved
Used by Permission

LINUS AND LUCY
from A CHARLIE BROWN CHRISTMAS
By VINCE GUARALDI

Copyright © 1965 LEE MENDELSON FILM PRODUCTIONS, INC.
Copyright Renewed
International Copyright Secured   All Rights Reserved

ALL ABOUT THAT BASS
Words and Music by KEVIN KADISH and MEGHAN TRAINOR

Copyright © 2015 Rezven Music, Year Of The Dog Music and MTrain Music
All Rights for Rezven Music Administered by Amplified Administration
All Rights for Year Of The Dog Music and MTrain Music Administered by Downtown Music Publishing LLC
All Rights Reserved   Used by Permission

Legato

An articulation indicating to play smooth and connected.

Slur

Connects two or more notes of any pitch. A **slur** indicates to play with a legato articulation.

> **TOOLBOX TIP**
>
> **SLURRING**
>
> When you slur notes on a trombone, the articulation starts with the middle of the tongue, like you are saying "doo," rather than "tah." The tongue should start the note at the exact moment the slide arrives in the new position to make the notes appear connected.
>
> The same tonguing approach is used with legato playing.

DANSE BACCHANALE
from SAMSON AND DELILA
By CAMILLE SAINT-SAËNS

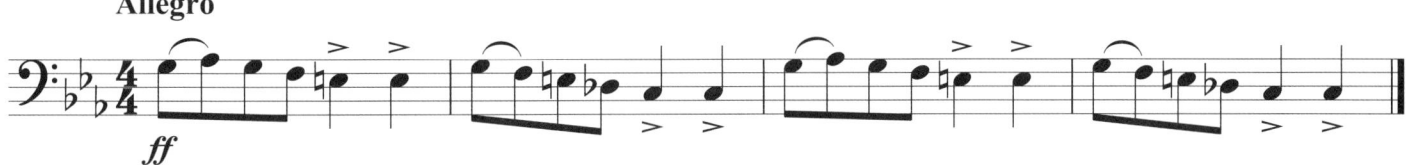

Copyright © 2022 by HAL LEONARD LLC
International Copyright Secured   All Rights Reserved

OH, PRETTY WOMAN
Words and Music by ROY ORBISON and BILL DEES

Copyright © 1964 Sony Music Publishing LLC, R Key Darkus Publishing, Orbi Lee Publishing, Barbara Orbison Music Publishing and Roys Boys LLC
Copyright Renewed
All Rights on behalf of Sony Music Publishing LLC Administered by Sony Music Publishing LLC, 424 Church Street, Suite 1200, Nashville, TN 37219
All Rights on behalf of R Key Darkus Publishing, Orbi Lee Publishing, Barbara Orbison Music Publishing and Roys Boys LLC Administered by Songs Of Kobalt Music Publishing
International Copyright Secured   All Rights Reserved

STAND BY ME
Words and Music by JERRY LEIBER, MIKE STOLLER and BEN E. KING

Copyright © 1961 Sony Music Publishing LLC
Copyright Renewed
All Rights Administered by Sony Music Publishing LLC, 424 Church Street, Suite 1200, Nashville, TN 37219
International Copyright Secured   All Rights Reserved

Sometimes two of the same notes are slurred together. Use a light "doo" tongue to make them smooth, but not tied to each other.

YESTERDAY

Words and Music by JOHN LENNON and PAUL McCARTNEY

Copyright © 1965 Sony Music Publishing LLC
Copyright Renewed
All Rights Administered by Sony Music Publishing LLC, 424 Church Street, Suite 1200, Nashville, TN 37219
International Copyright Secured   All Rights Reserved

Pentatonic Scale

A scale consisting of five notes. This scale produces melodies that are often associated with ancient civilizations and are commonly found in rock and blues music.

> **TOOLBOX TIP**
>
> **KEY SIGNATURES**
>
> The key signature indicates which scale is used to develop the melody. This minimizes the number of accidentals that would be notated in a piece of music.
>
> Key signatures sometimes include flats and sharps that are not written in the song.

COLORS OF THE WIND
from POCAHONTAS
Music by ALAN MENKEN • Lyrics by STEPHEN SCHWARTZ

© 1995 Wonderland Music Company, Inc. and Walt Disney Music Company
All Rights Reserved. Used by Permission.

UNDER THE BRIDGE
Words and Music by ANTHONY KIEDIS, FLEA, JOHN FRUSCIANTE and CHAD SMITH

© 1991 MOEBETOBLAME MUSIC
All Rights Reserved Used by Permission

Glissando

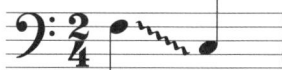

A musical effect in which the slide is moved without tonging to create a sliding or "smearing" sound. The first note is tongued in a **glissando**.

> **TOOLBOX TIP**
>
> **DIXIELAND MUSIC**
>
> **Dixieland** developed as a style of jazz in the early 20th century and was influenced by a combination of ragtime, blues, gospel and military bands. The trombone is an integral part of Dixieland music, especially known for incorporating glissandos into the melodic material.
>
> Some of the more famous Dixieland trombonists include Kid Ory and Jack Teagarden.

WHEN THE SAINTS GO MARCHING IN
Music by JAMES M. BLACK

Copyright © 2022 by HAL LEONARD LLC
International Copyright Secured   All Rights Reserved

Scoop

Sliding up to the pitch, starting 1-2 positions below the written note. The length of the scoop is usually determined by the speed of the music.

SCOOPING EXERCISE

Slow scoop

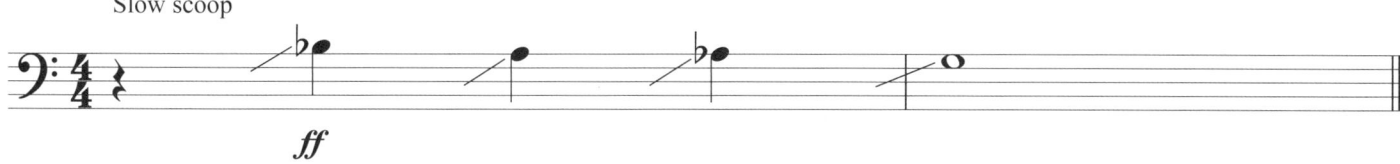

69

TOOLBOX TIP

PLUNGER MUTES

Plunger mutes are often used in jazz and occasionally in contemporary music. When the music is marked with a "+", place the plunger mute over most of the bell to muffle the sound. When the music is marked with a "o", move the plunger away from the bell while playing.

By keeping the bottom of the plunger against the bottom of the bell, it is much easier to alternate between open (o) and closed (+). You can use your hand if you don't have a plunger mute.

SUMMERTIME
from PORGY AND BESS®
Music and Lyrics by GEORGE GERSHWIN, DUBOSE and DOROTHY HEYWARD and IRA GERSHWIN

© 1935 (Renewed) NOKAWI MUSIC, FRANKIE G. SONGS, DUBOSE AND DOROTHY HEYWARD MEMORIAL FUND PUBLISHING and IRA GERSHWIN MUSIC
All Rights for NOKAWI MUSIC Administered in the U.S. by STEVE PETER MUSIC
All Rights for FRANKIE G. SONGS and DUBOSE AND DOROTHY HEYWARD MEMORIAL FUND PUBLISHING Administered by DOWNTOWN DLJ SONGS
All Rights for IRA GERSHWIN MUSIC Administered by WC MUSIC CORP.
All Rights Reserved   Used by Permission

TOOLBOX TIP

FLUTTER TONGUING

Flutter tonguing is a technique that is used in jazz, funk and contemporary pieces of music. The same principles used to roll the "R" sound in the Spanish language apply to the flutter tongue. Allow the tip of the tongue to vibrate as fast as possible, as if you were rolling your "R" sound while buzzing in the mouthpiece. This technique can also be incorporated with the plunger mute. It can be notated in the music as:

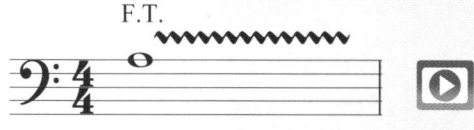

Tenuto

An articulation that indicates the note should be held its full value.

NEW NOTE: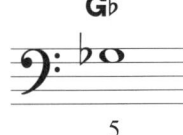

IT DON'T MEAN A THING
(IF IT AIN'T GOT THAT SWING)
Words and Music by DUKE ELLINGTON and IRVING MILLS

Copyright © 1932 Sony Music Publishing LLC and EMI Mills Music, Inc. in the U.S.A.
Copyright Renewed
All Rights on behalf of Sony Music Publishing LLC Administered by Sony Music Publishing LLC, 424 Church Street, Suite 1200, Nashville, TN 37219
Rights for the world outside the U.S.A. Administered by EMI Mills Music, Inc. (Publishing) and Alfred Music (Print)
International Copyright Secured   All Rights Reserved

IRON MAN
Words and Music by FRANK IOMMI, JOHN OSBOURNE, WILLIAM WARD and TERENCE BUTLER

© Copyright 1970 (Renewed) and 1974 (Renewed) Westminster Music Ltd., London, England
TRO - Essex Music International, Inc., New York, controls all publication rights for the U.S.A. and Canada
International Copyright Secured
All Rights Reserved Including Public Performance For Profit
Used by Permission

SMOKE ON THE WATER
Words and Music by RITCHIE BLACKMORE, IAN GILLAN, ROGER GLOVER, JON LORD and IAN PAICE

Copyright © 1972 B. Feldman & Co. Ltd.
Copyright Renewed
All Rights Administered by Sony Music Publishing LLC, 424 Church Street, Suite 1200, Nashville, TN 37219
International Copyright Secured   All Rights Reserved

pp **Pianissimo:** Very soft

Ritardando
Gradually slow down. Often abbreviated in music as "rit."

Fermata
Hold for a longer unspecified amount of time.

> **TOOLBOX — FERMATA**
> When playing a note with a **fermata**, hold the note longer than its usual duration. Fermatas can aslo be placed over rests.

MORE THAN WORDS
Words and Music by NUNO BETTENCOURT and GARY CHERONE

Copyright © 1990 COLOR ME BLIND MUSIC
All Rights Administered by ALMO MUSIC CORP.
All Rights Reserved   Used by Permission

72

THE WAY YOU LOOK TONIGHT
from SWING TIME
Words by DOROTHY FIELDS • Music by JEROME KERN

Moderato

IN THE HALL OF THE MOUNTAIN KING
from PEER GYNT
By EDVARD GRIEG

Copyright © 2022 by HAL LEONARD LLC
International Copyright Secured   All Rights Reserved

MORNING HAS BROKEN
Words by ELEANOR FARJEON • Music by CAT STEVENS

Copyright © 1971 Cat Music Ltd. and BMG Rights Management (UK) Ltd.
Copyright Renewed
All Rights Administered by BMG Rights Management (US) LLC
All Rights Reserved   Used by Permission

B♭ BLUES SCALE

Triplets

Three notes of equal length that are played in the duration that two of those notes would normally be played.

Quarter note triplets

2 beats   2 beats

Eighth note triplets

1 beat   1 beat

Triplets are often counted like this:

trip - a - let   trip - a - let

SEVEN NATION ARMY
Words and Music by JACK WHITE

Copyright © 2003 SONGS OF UNIVERSAL, INC. and PEPPERMINT STRIPE MUSIC
All Rights Administered by SONGS OF UNIVERSAL, INC.
All Rights Reserved   Used by Permission

SPONGEBOB SQUAREPANTS THEME SONG
from SPONGEBOB SQUAREPANTS
Words and Music by MARK HARRISON, BLAISE SMITH,
STEVE M. HILLENBURG and DEREK DRYMON

Copyright © 2001 TUNES BY NICKELODEON, INC.
All Rights Administered by UNIVERSAL MUSIC CORP.
All Rights Reserved   Used by Permission

CHARIOTS OF FIRE
from CHARIOTS OF FIRE
By VANGELIS

I'LL BE THERE
Words and Music by BERRY GORDY JR., HAL DAVIS, WILLIE HUTCH and BOB WEST

Swing

A musical style, or feeling where eighth notes are not even in length. The first of a group of two eighth notes will feel slightly longer than the second note. This feeling is best described as a triplet, where the first eighth note receives two of the triplet's beats, and the second eighth note receives the final beat of the triplet. These notes are generally smooth, and the style is best imitated by saying "doo-bah, doo-bah, doo-bah, doo-bah."

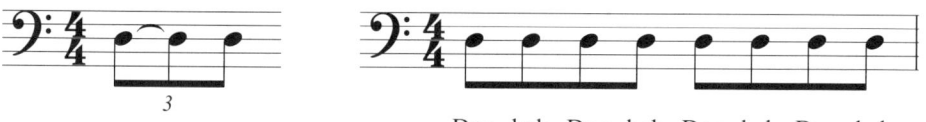

RAINDROPS KEEP FALLIN' ON MY HEAD
from BUTCH CASSIDY AND THE SUNDANCE KID
Lyrics by HAL DAVID • Music by BURT BACHARACH

Copyright © 1969 BMG Rights Management (UK) Ltd., New Hidden Valley Music Co. and WC Music Corp.
Copyright Renewed
All Rights Administered by BMG Rights Management (US) LLC
All Rights Reserved Used by Permission

THE WANDERER
Words and Music by ERNEST MARESCA

Copyright © 2022 by HAL LEONARD LLC
International Copyright Secured All Rights Reserved

SWEET CAROLINE

Words and Music by NEIL DIAMOND

Copyright © 1969 STONEBRIDGE-MUSIC, INC.
Copyright Renewed
All Rights Administered by UNIVERSAL TUNES
All Rights Reserved   Used by Permission

LESSON 8:
Vibrato

Vibrato
Rapid bending of a pitch to produce a better tone through expression.

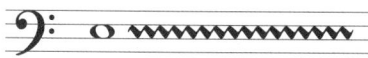

The depth of the vibrato will almost reach the notes one half step higher and lower than the written pitch.

The speed of the vibrato is based upon the pitch that is being played. Notes that are a lower frequency have a slower wavelength, therefore the vibrato would be slower. Higher notes require faster vibrato.

> **TROMBONE TALK: VIBRATO**
> Playing with vibrato can be accomplished by moving your jaw slightly as if you are chewing gum, or saying, "wah, wah, wah, wah…" (like trying to steam up a window).

VIBRATO EXERCISES – PULSING & BENDING

Play the whole note written, pulsing/bending the pitch at the speed of the stemmed notes. Do not tongue the stemmed notes; this is the speed the notes should bend. You are encouraged to watch the video for a demonstration.

Repeat the exercise on several pitches of your choice. Remember, the lower the note, the slower the pitch bend (vibrato).

Practice vibrato on the longer notes in "Somewhere Out There."

SOMEWHERE OUT THERE
from AN AMERICAN TAIL
Music by BARRY MANN and JAMES HORNER • Lyric by CYNTHIA WEIL

Copyright © 1986 USI A MUSIC PUBLISHING and USI B MUSIC PUBLISHING
All Rights Controlled and Administered by UNIVERSAL MUSIC CORP. and SONGS OF UNIVERSAL, INC.
All Rights Reserved   Used by Permission

> **TROMBONE TALK: SLIDE VIBRATO**
>
> Some jazz pieces of music call for a technique where the trombone slide is moved a very small distance back and forth quickly. This is known as **slide vibrato**. It is not usually notated in the music. This technique is left to the performer for their own interpretation.

UNFORGETTABLE
Words and Music by IRVING GORDON

Copyright © 1951 by Unforgettable Standards
Copyright Renewed
All Rights in the United States, its possessions and territories Administered by Songs Of Peer, Ltd.
All Rights outside the U.S. Administered by Bourne Co.
International Copyright Secured   All Rights Reserved

TROMBONE TALK: SLIDE POSITION

There are no "guaranteed" correct placements for each slide position. Playing the trombone in tune requires constant listening and adjusting. Even the same note repeated several times might need slight slide adjustments up or down to be in tune based on the music.

Trombone is one of the easiest instruments to tune because of the slide, and yet one of the hardest instruments to play in tune - there are no "locked" positions on the slide except first position!

THE LION SLEEPS TONIGHT

New Lyrics and Revised Music by GEORGE DAVID WEISS, LUIGI CREATORE and HUGO PERETTI

Copyright © 1961 Abilene Music, Luigi Creatore Music, HJP Music and Hugo Peretti Music
Copyright Renewed
All Rights for Abilene Music and Luigi Creatore Music Administered by Concord Sounds c/o Concord Music Publishing
All Rights for HJP Music and Hugo Peretti Music Administered by Steve Peter Music
All Rights Reserved   Used by Permission

LESSON 9:
Lip Slurs

Playing more than one note in the same position without tonguing more than the first note is called a **lip slur**. For example, you have learned how to play 3 notes in 1st position to this point (low B♭, F, high B♭).

However, if you add a slur to these notes and only tongue the first pitch, it is a lip slur.

Lip slurs require a rapid change in air speed to get the notes to change pitch without moving the slide. To get higher notes to sound, your air speed must increase as your aperture gets smaller. This pressurizes your air and allows the higher notes in that position to speak. Notes that are in the same slide position but have different pitches are part of the **harmonic series**. The individual notes in one position are called **partials.** The example below shows the first eight partials of the harmonic series in first position.

A trombone has an unlimited range of notes in any given slide position. As the notes get higher in the harmonic series, the interval between the notes becomes closer together.

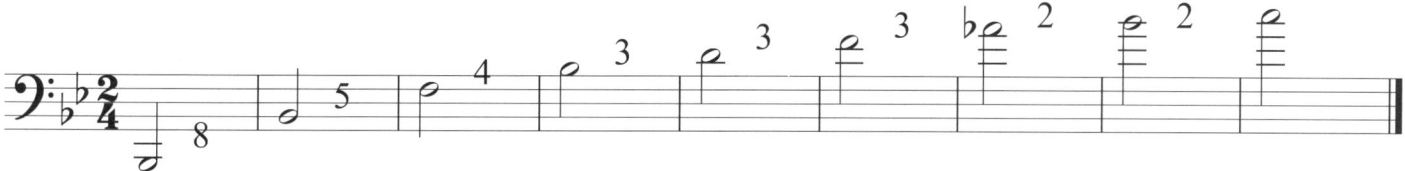

As you can see in the diagram above, each successive note has a smaller interval of distance to the next higher note. All of these pitches (and more) can be played in first position on the trombone. Accomplished trombonists have a range of over 3 octaves.

Your range will increase dramatically by spending time daily on lip slurs. These are the building blocks to success on your instrument. The next pages contain lip slur and harmonic series exercises that have been created to improve your ability to play even higher and lower on the trombone.

All exercises should completed in ALL seven positions. As you move the slide out, each lip slur will require more air to produce a good, characteristic trombone sound. This is because you are making the instrument longer by moving the outer slide further from the mouthpiece.

NOTE: These exercises contain notes you have not learned, but they can be played by following the positions written above the beginning of each lip slur. All notes included in the slur are in the same position.

1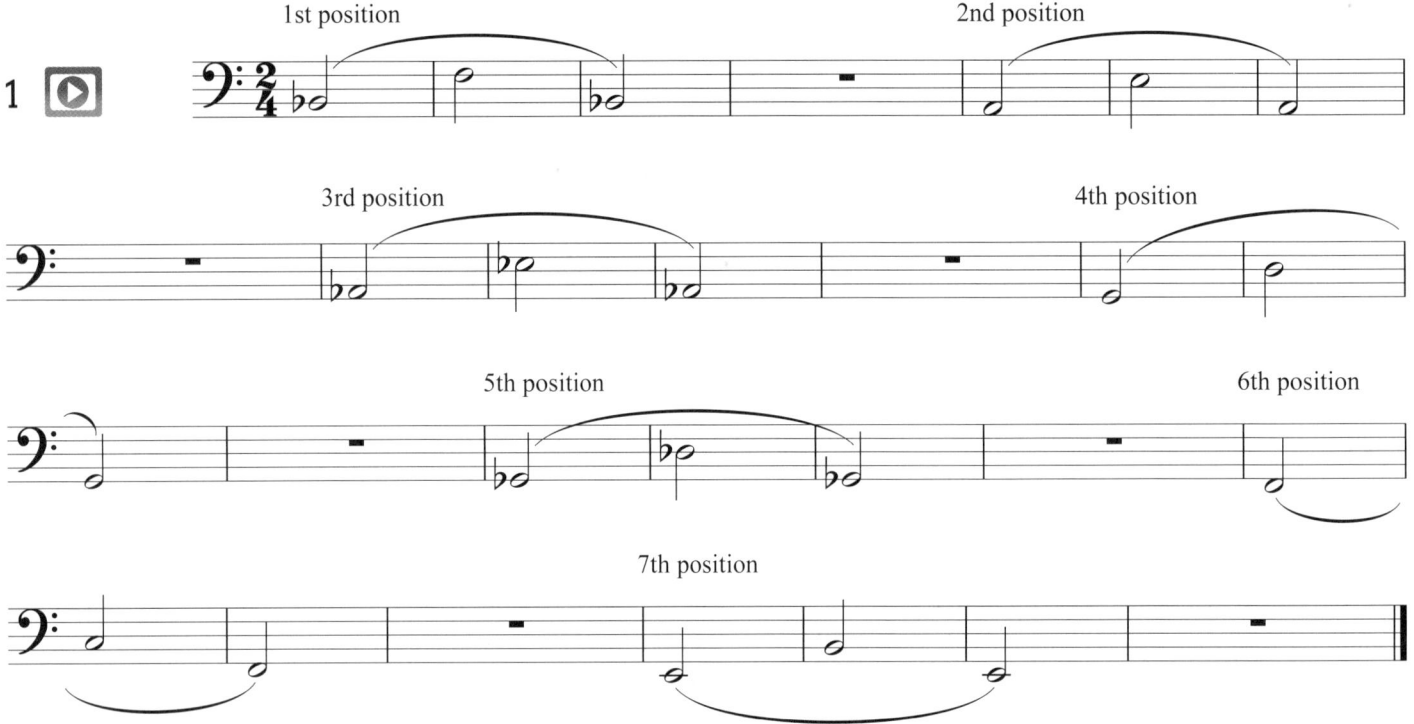

The next lip slur follows the same pattern but begins one **partial** higher.

2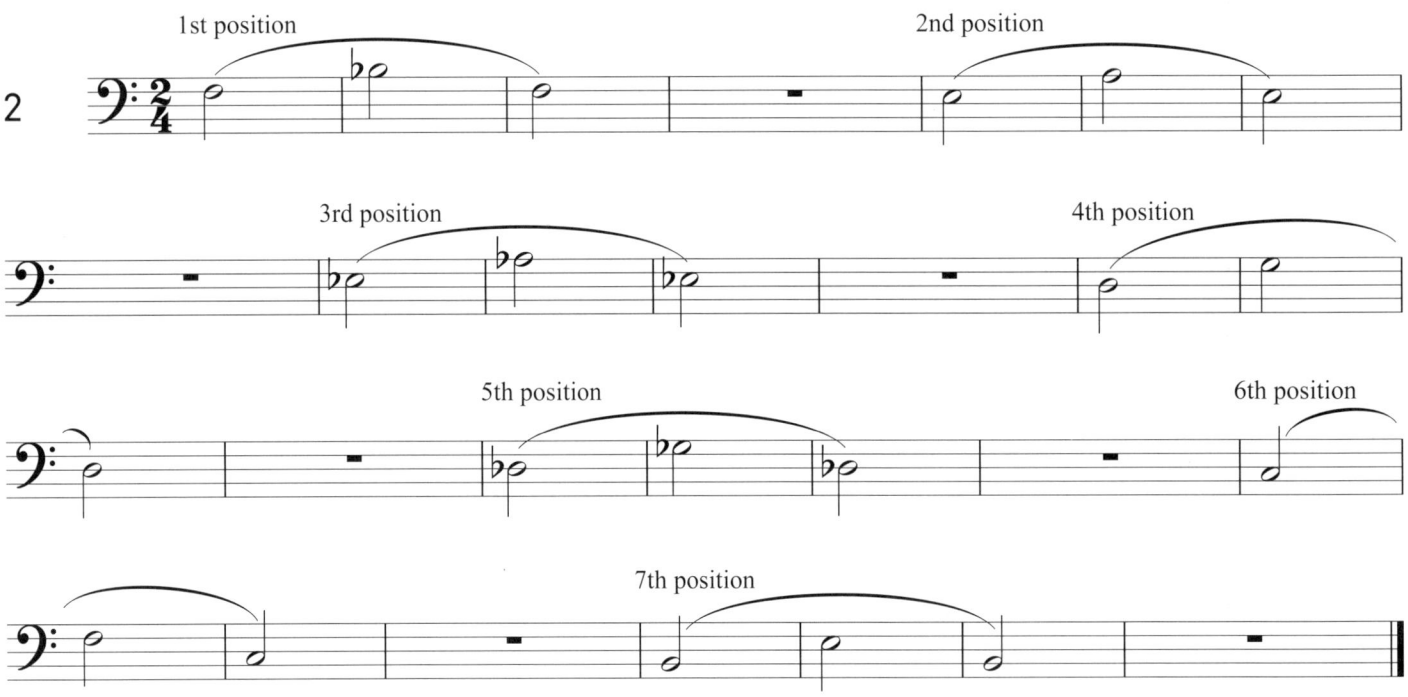

These (and all lip slurs) can be played at any speed. Begin with long tones, focusing on making the notes change ONLY by changing your airspeed, NOT by using your tongue. Once you have control over the lip slurs, you can begin to play them faster for greater technical control and increased difficulty. The smoother you can make the slur, the more your technique will improve.

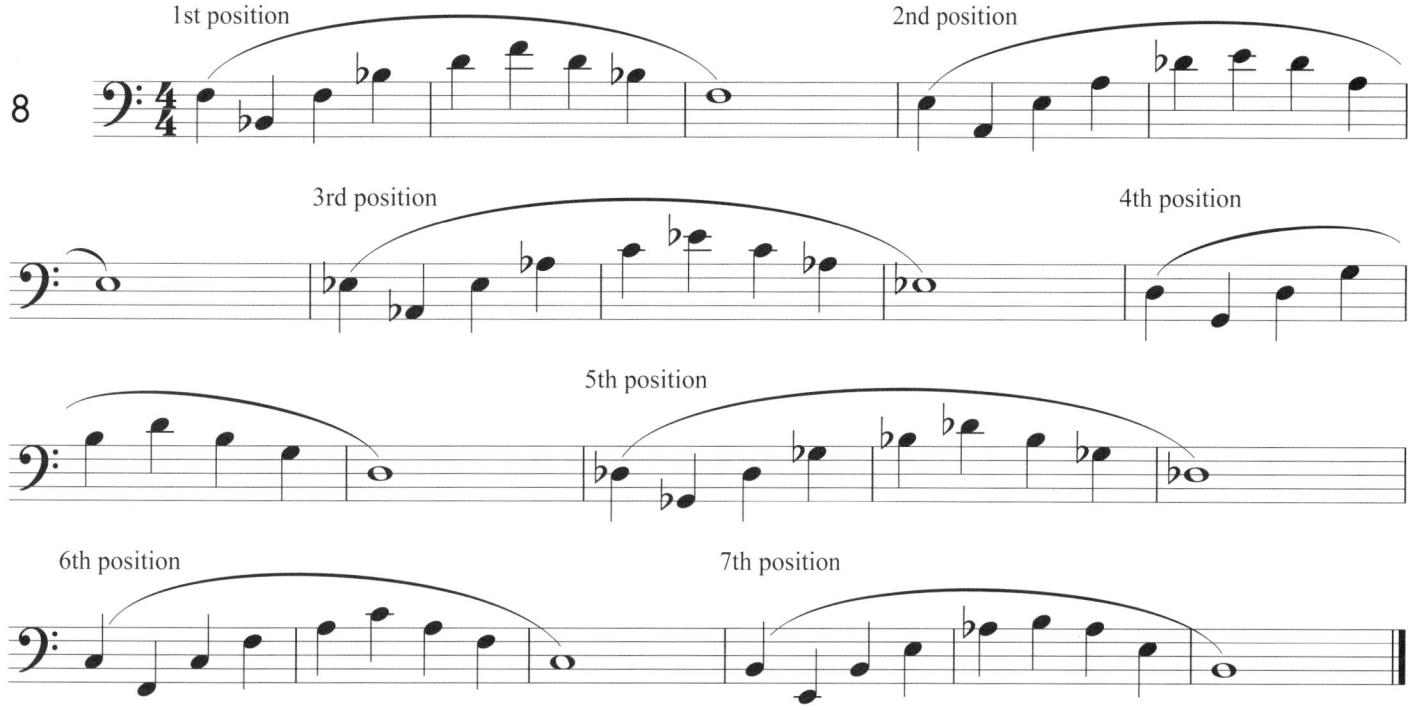

Time Signature

6 = 6 beats in each measure
8 = eighth note ♪ receives one beat

6/8 time is often broken into two beats, with each beat comprised of three eighth notes. This time signature gives the music a bouncy feel as the first and fourth count receive the most emphasis, or weight. It can be counted in six as well, but fast tempos often make that much more challenging.

> **COUNTING 6/8 TIME BREAKDOWN**
> Eighth note: one count (often written in groups of three)
> Quarter note: two counts
> Dotted quarter note: three counts
> Dotted half note: six counts
>
> **COMMON 6/8 RHYTHMS**

ITSY BITSY SPIDER
Traditional

DOTTED QUARTER REST
The dot adds half of the value of the rest to the existing rest. In 6/8 time, the dotted quarter rest receives three beats of silence because an eighth rest receives one beat.

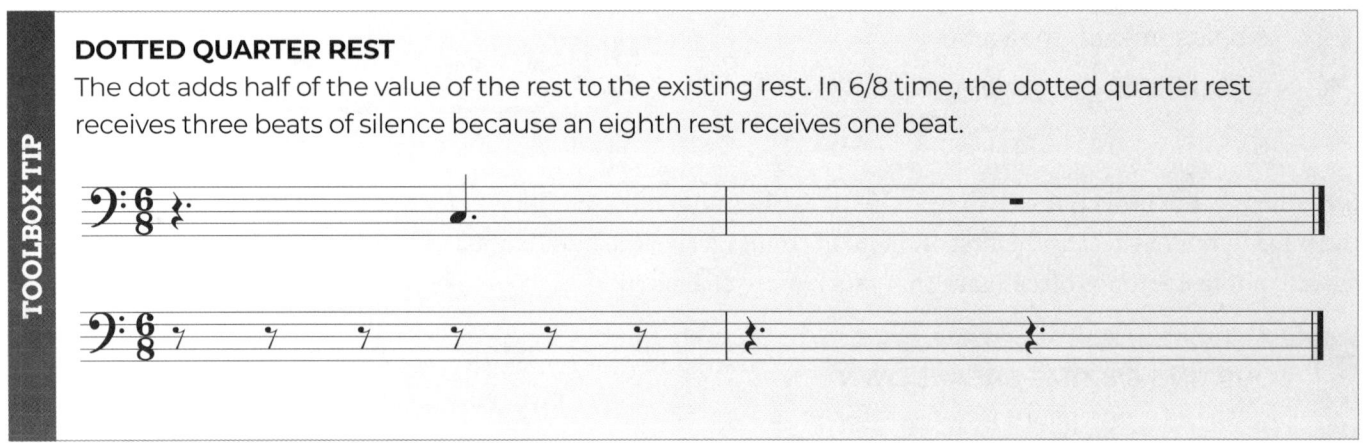

ROW, ROW, ROW YOUR BOAT
Traditional

ADDAMS FAMILY THEME
Theme from the TV Show and Movie
Music and Lyrics by VIC MIZZY

Slow 6/8 Time

While fast 6/8 time is counted in two, slow 6/8 time is counted in six.

NEW NOTE:

> **TOOLBOX**
>
> **TEMPOS**
> Often in popular music, tempos are written in contemporary terms, rather than in Italian as had been done with earlier styles of music. Rather than writing Allegro, they might write "Driving Rock" or "Fast." Moderato could be notated as "Freely," Adagio could be "Slowly."

YOU AND ME
Words and Music by JUDE COLE and JASON WADE

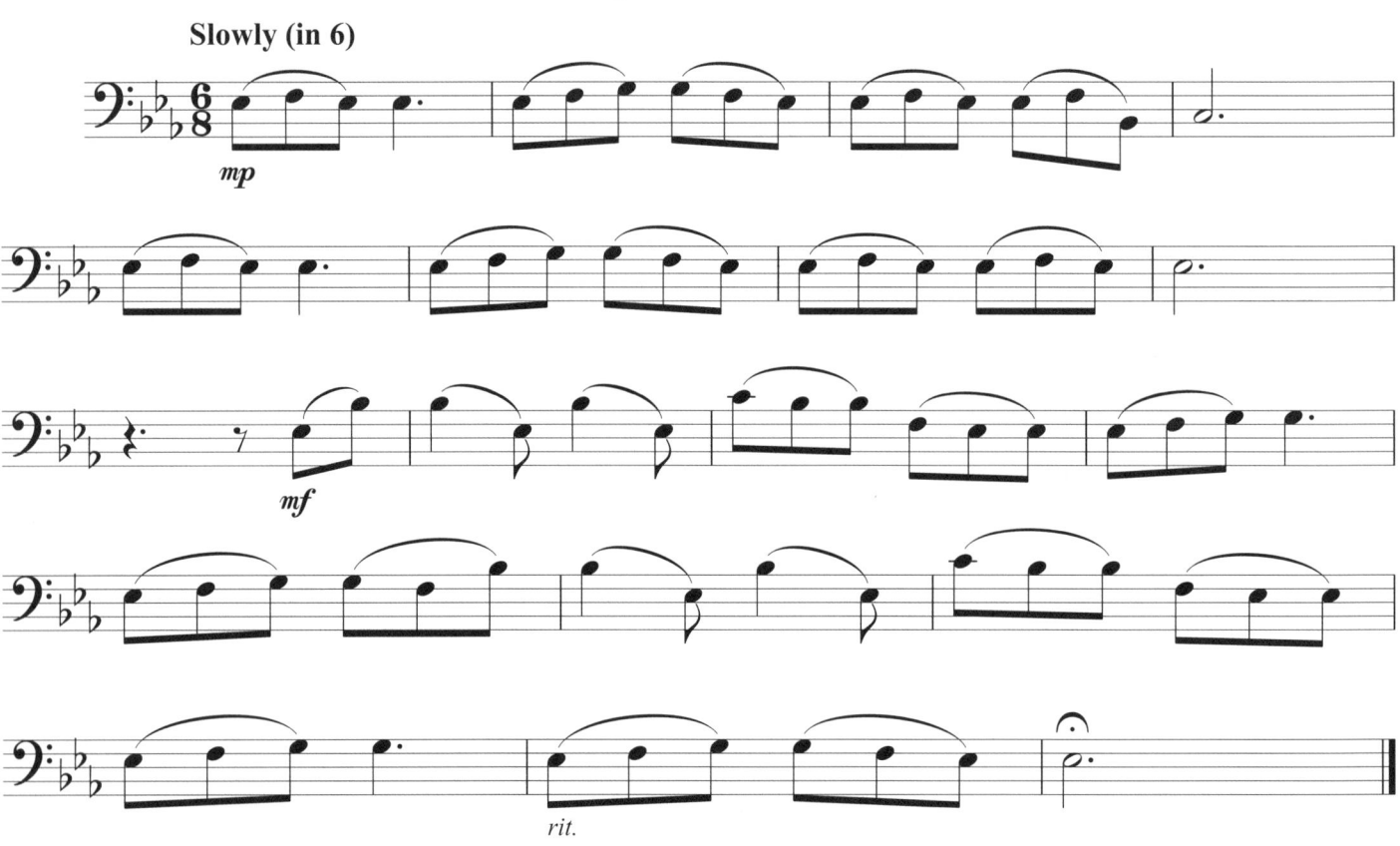

Copyright © 2005 Jude Cole Music and G-Chills Music
All Rights Reserved   Used by Permission

Remember: To play a higher note, you will need your aperture to be smaller and your air speed to increase! Your air should be pointed down in the mouthpiece.

PERFECT
Words and Music by ED SHEERAN

EINE KLEINE NACHTMUSIK ("SERENADE"), FIRST MOVEMENT EXCERPT

By WOLFGANG AMADEUS MOZART

Copyright © 2022 by HAL LEONARD LLC
International Copyright Secured   All Rights Reserved

NEW NOTE:

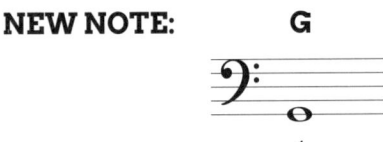

OYE COMO VA

Words and Music by TITO PUENTE

Copyright © 1962 EMI Full Keel Music
Copyright Renewed
All Rights Administered by Sony Music Publishing LLC, 424 Church Street, Suite 1200, Nashville, TN 37219
International Copyright Secured   All Rights Reserved

TOOLBOX TIPS

D.C. al Fine

When you reach the D.C. al Fine, return back to the beginning of the piece and stop playing when you reach the Fine. You do not stop at the Fine the first time.

When the music indicates D.C. al Fine (with repeat), all repeats that appear after returning to the beginning of the song should be played.

Da Capo (D.C.): From the beginning   **Fine:** The end

UNCHAINED MELODY
from the Motion Picture UNCHAINED
Lyric by HY ZARET • Music by ALEX NORTH

© 1955 (Renewed) North Melody Publishing (SESAC) and HZUM Publishing (SESAC) c/o Unchained Melody Publishing, LLC
All Rights Reserved   Used by Permission

WE'RE NOT GONNA TAKE IT
Words and Music by DANIEL DEE SNIDER

Copyright © 1984 by Universal Music - Z Melodies and Snidest Music
All Rights in the United States Administered by Universal Music - Z Melodies
International Copyright Secured All Rights Reserved

GIVE ME THAT OLD TIME RELIGION
Traditional

Copyright © 2022 by HAL LEONARD LLC
International Copyright Secured All Rights Reserved

Sixteenth Note

Count: 1   e   &   a

Count: 1 e & a   2 e & a   3 e & a   4 e & a

A sixteenth note receives 1/4 of a beat of sound. Often, they are in groups of two or four notes.

It would take 16 sixteenth notes to fill this measure in 4/4 time.

Notice the sixteenth notes in the next song are a lip slur in second position!

THE GOOD, THE BAD AND THE UGLY (MAIN TITLE)
from THE GOOD, THE BAD AND THE UGLY
By ENNIO MORRICONE

© 1966, 1968 (Renewed) EDIZIONI EUREKA (Italy)
All Rights Controlled and Administered by EMI UNART CATALOG INC. (Publishing) and ALFRED MUSIC (Print)
All Rights Reserved   Used by Permission

Sixteenth Note Variations

Many songs incorporate sixteenth notes, but use variations of sixteenth notes and eighth notes or rests. Some of the more common include

Count: 1   &   a   Count: 1   &   a   Count: 1   e   &   Count: 1   e   &
                                            (rest)   (rest)

ANOTHER ONE BITES THE DUST
Words and Music by JOHN DEACON

Copyright © 1980 Queen Music Ltd.
All Rights Administered by Sony Music Publishing LLC, 424 Church Street, Suite 1200, Nashville, TN 37219
International Copyright Secured   All Rights Reserved

UNDER PRESSURE

Words and Music by FREDDIE MERCURY, JOHN DEACON,
BRIAN MAY, ROGER TAYLOR and DAVID BOWIE

Copyright © 1981 EMI Music Publishing Ltd., Queen Music Ltd. and Tintoretto Music
All Rights on behalf of EMI Music Publishing Ltd. and Queen Music Ltd. Administered by Sony Music Publishing LLC, 424 Church Street, Suite 1200, Nashville, TN 37219
All Rights on behalf of Tintoretto Music Administered by RZO Music
International Copyright Secured   All Rights Reserved

LULLABY

By JOHANNES BRAHMS

Copyright © 2022 by HAL LEONARD LLC
International Copyright Secured   All Rights Reserved

WALK THIS WAY

Words and Music by STEVEN TYLER and JOE PERRY

Copyright © 1975 Music Of Stage Three
Copyright Renewed
All Rights Administered by Stage Three Music (US) Inc., a BMG Chrysalis company
All Rights Reserved   Used by Permission

ALL STAR
Words and Music by GREG CAMP

Copyright © 1999 Songs By Greg Camp and Squish Moth Music
All Rights Controlled and Administered by Spirit One Music
International Copyright Secured All Rights Reserved Used by Permission

SPINNING SONG
By ALBERT ELLMENREICH

Copyright © 2022 by HAL LEONARD LLC
International Copyright Secured All Rights Reserved

Dotted Eighth/Sixteenth

Count: 1 e & a
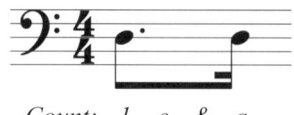
Count: 1 e & a

1/2 + 1/4 = 3/4 beat

Recall from earlier, the dot adds half of the value to the existing note. A dotted-eighth note is worth 3/4 of one beat.

New Style
Maestoso: Majestically

BRIDAL CHORUS
from LOHENGRIN
By Richard Wagner

Copyright © 2022 by HAL LEONARD LLC
International Copyright Secured   All Rights Reserved

FUNERAL MARCH
from PIANO SONATA IN B-FLAT MINOR, OP. 35
By FRYDERYK CHOPIN

Copyright © 2022 by HAL LEONARD LLC
International Copyright Secured   All Rights Reserved

EYE OF THE TIGER
Theme from ROCKY III
Words and Music by FRANK SULLIVAN and JIM PETERIK

Copyright © 1982 Sony Music Publishing LLC, Rude Music, Three Wise Boys LLC, WC Music Corp. and Easy Action Music
All Rights on behalf of Sony Music Publishing LLC, Rude Music and Three Wise Boys LLC Administered by Sony Music Publishing LLC, 424 Church Street, Suite 1200, Nashville, TN 37219
All Rights on behalf of Easy Action Music Administered by WC Music Corp.
International Copyright Secured   All Rights Reserved

IF YOU'RE HAPPY AND YOU KNOW IT
Words and Music by L. SMITH

Copyright © 2022 by HAL LEONARD LLC
International Copyright Secured   All Rights Reserved

CENTERFOLD
Words and Music by SETH JUSTMAN

Copyright © 1981 Center City Music and Pal-Park Music
All Rights for Center City Music Administered Worldwide by Kobalt Songs Music Publishing
All Rights for Pal-Park Music Administered by Almo Music Corp.
All Rights Reserved   Used by Permission

Multiple Measure Rest

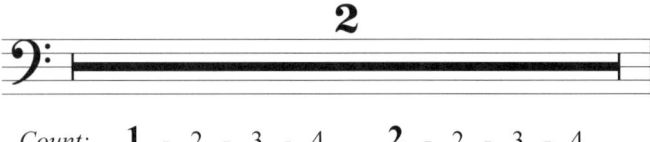

Count: **1** - 2 - 3 - 4   **2** - 2 - 3 - 4

When the music dictates rests that are beyond one measure in length, they may be written as a single measure with a number notated above. That number indicates the quantity of full measures to rest.

NEW NOTE: B

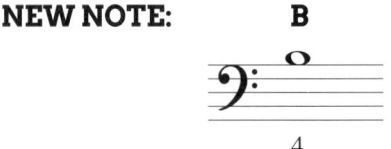

C MAJOR SCALE

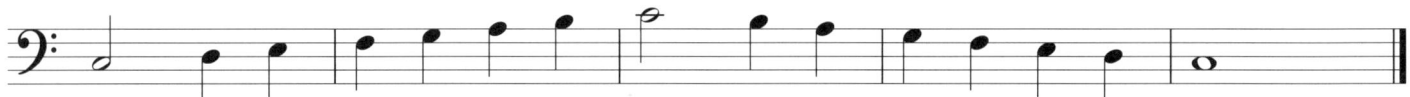

I WISH
Words and Music by STEVIE WONDER

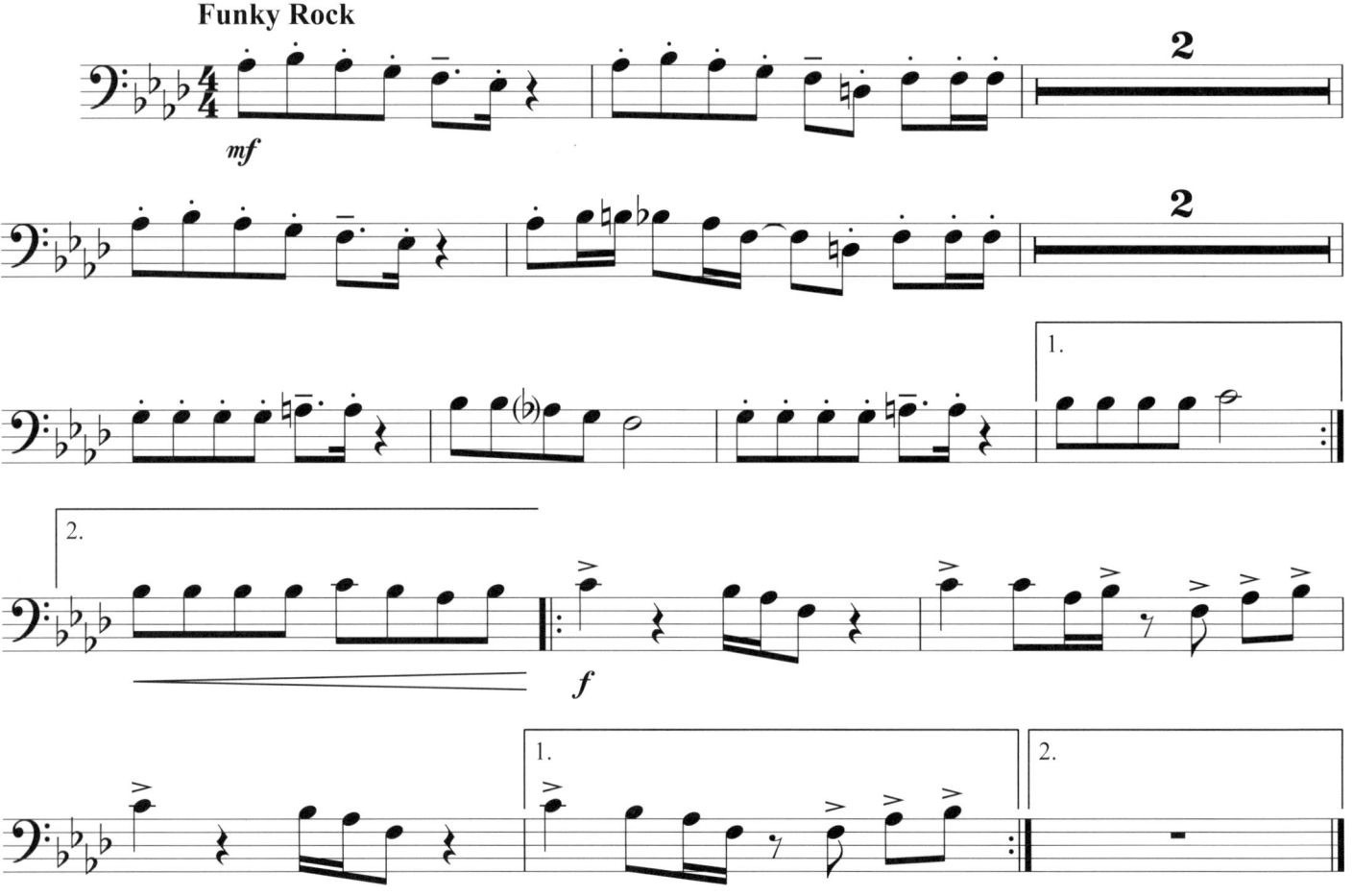

Copyright © 1976 Jobete Music Co., Inc. and Black Bull Music
Copyright Renewed
All Rights Administered by Sony Music Publishing LLC, 424 Church Street, Suite 1200, Nashville, TN 37219
International Copyright Secured   All Rights Reserved

TOOLBOX TIPS

a tempo – return to the original tempo

Rallentando (rall.) – gradually slow down (similar to Ritardando)

Molto ritardando (molto rit.) – gradually slow down very much

The temporary speeding up and slowing down within a piece of music is called **rubato**. Composers will often give suggestions where the tempo should fluctuate by notating *rit.*, *rall.*, and *a tempo* within the piece.

THAT'S AMORÉ (THAT'S LOVE)
from the Paramount Picture THE CADDY
Words by JACK BROOKS · Music by HARRY WARREN

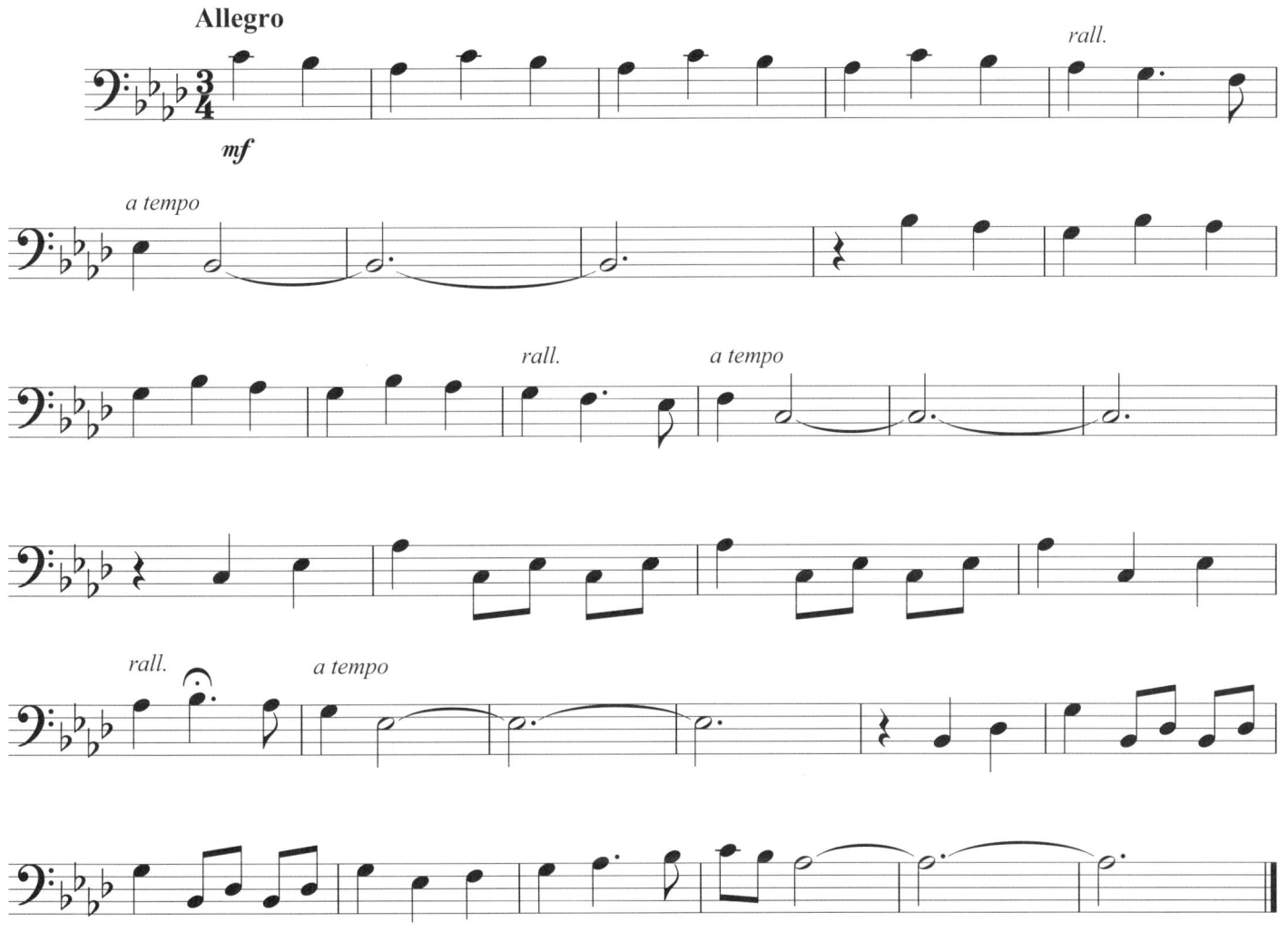

Copyright © 1953 Sony Music Publishing LLC and Four Jays Music
Copyright Renewed
All Rights on behalf of Sony Music Publishing LLC Administered by Sony Music Publishing LLC, 424 Church Street, Suite 1200, Nashville, TN 37219
International Copyright Secured   All Rights Reserved

DANNY BOY

Words by FREDERICK EDWARD WEATHERLY
Traditional Irish Folk Melody

Copyright © 2022 by HAL LEONARD LLC
International Copyright Secured   All Rights Reserved

I STILL HAVEN'T FOUND WHAT I'M LOOKING FOR

Words and Music by U2

Copyright © 1987 UNIVERSAL MUSIC PUBLISHING INTERNATIONAL B.V.
All Rights in the United States and Canada Controlled and Administered by UNIVERSAL - POLYGRAM INTERNATIONAL PUBLISHING, INC.
All Rights Reserved   Used by Permission

OVER THE RAINBOW
from THE WIZARD OF OZ
Music by HAROLD ARLEN • Lyric by E.Y. "YIP" HARBURG

© 1938 (Renewed) METRO-GOLDWYN-MAYER INC.
© 1939 (Renewed) EMI FEIST CATALOG INC.
All Rights Administered by EMI FEIST CATALOG INC. (Publishing) and ALFRED MUSIC (Print)
All Rights Reserved   Used by Permission

TOOLBOX TIPS

PHRASE

A musical sentence, often 2 or 4 measures long.

Follow the direction of the notes to make your phrase more musical. If the notes go higher, you could add a **crescendo**. If the notes go lower, you may want to add a **decrescendo**. The goal in music is to add your own subtle changes to dynamics and tempo.

This is called **interpretation**.

POLKA DOTS AND MOONBEAMS
Words by JOHNNY BURKE • Music by JIMMY VAN HEUSEN

Copyright © 1939 by Bourne Co. (ASCAP), Marke-Music Publishing Co., Inc., Reganesque Music Company, My Dad's Songs, Inc. and Pocketful Of Dreams Music Publishing
Copyright Renewed
All Rights for Marke-Music Publishing Co., Inc. Administered by WC Music Corp.
All Rights for Reganesque Music Company Administered by Spirit Two Music, Inc.
All Rights for My Dad's Songs, Inc. and Pocketful Of Dreams Music Publishing Administered by Songs Of Mojo Two LLC
International Copyright Secured   All Rights Reserved

Keep each group of slurs smooth to make a musical **phrase**. Add dynamic contrast and slight tempo changes to make this your own interpretation of the music.

WONDERFUL TONIGHT
Words and Music by ERIC CLAPTON

Copyright © 1977 by Eric Patrick Clapton
Copyright Renewed
International Copyright Secured   All Rights Reserved

Marcato Accent

A **marcato accent** begins with a strong attack, followed by a decay in sound. There should be a small amount of space (silence) between these notes.

DON'T STOP BELIEVIN'
Words and Music by STEVE PERRY, NEAL SCHON and JONATHAN CAIN

Copyright © 1981 Lacey Boulevard Music (BMI) and Weed-High Nightmare Music (BMI)
All Rights for Weed-High Nightmare Music Administered by Wixen Music Publishing Inc.
International Copyright Secured   All Rights Reserved

TOOLBOX TIPS

D.C. al Coda

When you reach the **D.C. al Coda**, return back to the beginning of the piece and play until you reach the "To Coda" marking in the music. Jump down to the Coda (usually at the end of the piece) and play to the end of the song.

Coda: The conclusion ⨁   **To Coda** ⨁

STRANGERS IN THE NIGHT
adapted from A MAN COULD GET KILLED
Words by CHARLES SINGLETON and EDDIE SNYDER • Music by BERT KAEMPFERT

Copyright © 1966 SONGS OF UNIVERSAL, INC. and SCREEN GEMS-EMI MUSIC INC.
Copyright Renewed
All Rights for the World Controlled and Administered by SONGS OF UNIVERSAL, INC.
All Rights Reserved   Used by Permission

TEARS IN HEAVEN

Words and Music by ERIC CLAPTON and WILL JENNINGS

Copyright © 1992 by E.C. Music Ltd. and Blue Sky Rider Songs
All Rights for Blue Sky Rider Songs Administered by Irving Music, Inc.
International Copyright Secured   All Rights Reserved

TROMBONE TALK: ALTERNATE POSITIONS

Some notes on a trombone can be played in more than one position. When a composer wants an **alternate position** to be used, the slide position will be marked above the note. This is often done for convenience and ease of playing.

NEW NOTE: B

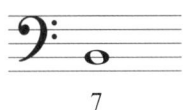

CAN'T HELP FALLING IN LOVE
from the Paramount Picture BLUE HAWAII
Words and Music by GEORGE DAVID WEISS, HUGO PERETTI and LUIGI CREATORE

Copyright © 1961 Gladys Music
Copyright Renewed
Extended U.S. Renewal and British Reversionary Territories Assigned to Abilene Music LLC, HJP Music, Hugo Peretti Music and Luigi Creatore Music
Administered in the United States during the Extended Renewal by Steve Peter Music
All Rights Reserved   Used by Permission

LESSON 10
Common Time and Cut Time

Common Time

Another way to notate 4/4 time.

I HEARD IT THROUGH THE GRAPEVINE
Words and Music by NORMAN J. WHITFIELD and BARRETT STRONG

Copyright © 1966 Stone Agate Music Inc.
Copyright Renewed
All Rights Administered by Sony Music Publishing LLC, 424 Church Street, Suite 1200, Nashville, TN 37219
International Copyright Secured   All Rights Reserved

NEW NOTE:

D
1

E♭
3

E♭ MAJOR SCALE

TOMORROW
from the Musical Production ANNIE

Lyric by MARTIN CHARNIN • Music by CHARLES STROUSE

© 1977 (Renewed) EDWIN H. MORRIS & COMPANY, A Division of MPL Music Publishing, Inc. and CHARLES STROUSE PUBLISHING
All Rights for CHARLES STROUSE PUBLISHING Administered by WC MUSIC CORP.
All Rights Reserved   Used by Permission

TROMBONE TALK: INSTRUMENT STAND

Sometimes the hardest part of learning an instrument is establishing a regular practice routine. If you have not already purchased a trombone stand for your instrument, do so and leave your instrument safely on the stand in an area that you travel frequently. This encourages more regular practicing, and will allow you to improve at a faster rate!

Copyright © 1971 Colgems-EMI Music Inc.
Copyright Renewed
All Rights Administered by Sony Music Publishing LLC, 424 Church Street, Suite 1200, Nashville, TN 37219
International Copyright Secured   All Rights Reserved

IMAGINE

Words and Music by JOHN LENNON

TOOLBOX TIPS

DOTTED EIGHTH/SIXTEENTH SUBDIVISION

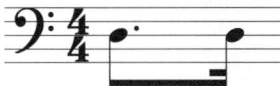

A common mistake among musicians is not properly subdividing note lengths. One of the most misplayed rhythms is the dotted eighth, sixteenth note. This rhythm is often played more in the style of the tied jazz triplet, or "swung" eighth notes.

INCORRECT   **CORRECT**

Break a quarter note into four equal subdivided beats. Sing this rhythm in your head and check to ensure that the dotted eighth note is receiving 3 of the 4 subdivided beats.

THE STAR-SPANGLED BANNER
Words by FRANCIS SCOTT KEY • Music by JOHN STAFFORD SMITH

Copyright © 2022 by HAL LEONARD LLC
International Copyright Secured   All Rights Reserved

March Tempo

Modern march tempo is 120 beats per minute (bpm). This speed was designed to align with the pace in which a group of soldiers would move together in step (two steps per second).

MARCH
from THE NUTCRACKER
By PYOTR IL'YICH TCHAIKOVSKY

Time Signature: Cut Time

 = 2 beats in each measure
= half note  receives one beat

Cut Time looks very similar to Common Time; however, the "C" is cut in half.

Cut time looks like 4/4 time, but the value of each beat is cut in half. Practice this piece as if it was written in 4/4, then play again with each note twice as fast – it will have the cut time feel.

SWEET HOME ALABAMA
Words and Music by RONNIE VAN ZANT, ED KING and GARY ROSSINGTON

Copyright © 1974 SONGS OF UNIVERSAL, INC., EMI LONGITUDE MUSIC, UNIVERSAL MUSIC CORP. and EMI FULL KEEL MUSIC
Copyright Renewed
All Rights for EMI LONGITUDE MUSIC Administered by SONGS OF UNIVERSAL, INC.
All Rights for EMI FULL KEEL MUSIC Administered by UNIVERSAL MUSIC CORP.
All Rights Reserved   Used by Permission

TROMBONE TALK: FAMOUS TROMBONE PLAYERS

The best way to learn a language is to hear others speaking that language. For this reason, having good models of tone and technique on the trombone is important. Find trombone players on recordings and imitate their sound. Some of the most famous trombone players include: J.J. Johnson, Bill Watrous, Christian Lindberg, Wycliffe Gordon, Carol Jarvis, Frank Rosolino, Joseph Alessi, Abbie Conant, Tommy Dorsey, Glenn Miller, Douglas Yeo, Charles Vernon and Urbie Green.

HERE'S THAT RAINY DAY
from CARNIVAL IN FLANDERS
Words by JOHNNY BURKE • Music by JIMMY VAN HEUSEN

Copyright © 1944, 1949, 1953 by Bourne Co. (ASCAP), Reganesque Music Company, My Dad's Songs, Pocketful Of Dreams Music Publishing and Marke-Music Publishing Co., Inc.
Copyright Renewed
All Rights for Reganesque Music Company in the United States Administered by Spirit Two Music, Inc.
All Rights for My Dad's Songs and Pocketful Of Dreams Music Publishing Administered by Songs Of Mojo Two LLC
All Rights for Marke-Music Publishing Co., Inc. Administered by WC Music Corp.
International Copyright Secured   All Rights Reserved

TOOLBOX TIPS

ENHARMONICS

When two notes have the same pitch but are written with different note names, they are **enharmonics**. Much like a homophone which has a different spelling but sounds the same, enharmonics are another way to write the same pitch differently.

A♯ = B♭   C♯ = D♭   D♯ = E♭   F♯ = G♭   G♯ = A♭

Since a sharp raises a note and a flat lowers a note, the next note higher written as a flat would be the same sound as the original note written as a sharp.

TROMBONE TALK: CHROMATIC SCALE

The chromatic scale uses every note name possible within an octave range. The word **chromatic** generally implies notes outside of the key signature. The chromatic scale is an ascending and descending scale moving up or down by a series of half steps.

Because each position on the trombone is a half-step apart, the chromatic scale is just a numerical pattern moving up or down (ex . *7th position, 6th position, 5th…etc.*)

B♭ CHROMATIC SCALE

HABANERA
from CARMEN
By GEORGES BIZET

Copyright © 2022 by HAL LEONARD LLC
International Copyright Secured   All Rights Reserved

TAKE ME OUT TO THE BALL GAME
Words by JACK NORWORTH • Music by ALBERT VON TILZER

Copyright © 2022 by HAL LEONARD LLC
International Copyright Secured   All Rights Reserved

TOOLBOX TIPS

ENHARMONIC REMINDER

Gb = F#

Ab = G#

Same pitch, different name

Same pitch, different name

DO NOTHIN' TILL YOU HEAR FROM ME
Words and Music by DUKE ELLINGTON and BOB RUSSELL

Copyright © 1943 Sony Music Publishing LLC and Music Sales Corporation
Copyright Renewed
All Rights on behalf of Sony Music Publishing LLC Administered by Sony Music Publishing LLC, 424 Church Street, Suite 1200, Nashville, TN 37219
International Copyright Secured   All Rights Reserved

119

> **TROMBONE TALK: TROMBONE PITCH TENDANCIES - 2ND & 5TH POSITION**
>
> Many trombonists will place their 2nd position too low and cause the note to sound as if it was played in 3rd position. Likewise, 5th position is often not far enough away from 4th position. Reach a little further when playing in 5th (D♭, G♭) and have very little of the inner slide showing when you are playing in 2nd position (A, E, high C♯, D♭, etc.). Of course, be prepared to adjust a little to play the note in tune!

GEORGIA ON MY MIND

Words by STUART GORRELL • Music by HOAGY CARMICHAEL

* Use 5th position

Copyright © 1930 by Peermusic III, Ltd.
Copyright Renewed
International Copyright Secured All Rights Reserved

TOOLBOX

TIME SIGNATURE/METER CHANGES

Sometimes music changes time signatures, or meter throughout the piece. When this occurs, continue counting at the same speed (unless otherwise indicated), only changing the number of beats in a measure.

TOOLBOX

D.S. al Fine

When you reach the **D.S. al Fine**, return back to the *Del Segno* (the sign) and play until you reach the *Fine* (the end).

*Helpful hint: D.S. is "da sign."

ALL YOU NEED IS LOVE
Words and Music by JOHN LENNON and PAUL McCARTNEY

Copyright © 1967 Sony Music Publishing LLC
Copyright Renewed
All Rights Administered by Sony Music Publishing LLC, 424 Church Street, Suite 1200, Nashville, TN 37219
International Copyright Secured All Rights Reserved

TOOLBOX

D.S. al Coda

When you reach the **D.S. al Coda**, return back to the **Del Segno**, or D.S. (the sign) in the piece and play until you reach the "To Coda" marking in the music. Jump down to the Coda (usually at the end of the piece) and play to the end of the song.

HEY JUDE

Words and Music by JOHN LENNON and PAUL McCARTNEY

Copyright © 1968 Sony Music Publishing LLC
Copyright Renewed
All Rights Administered by Sony Music Publishing LLC, 424 Church Street, Suite 1200, Nashville, TN 37219
International Copyright Secured   All Rights Reserved

TROMBONE TALK: CONTINUING YOUR JOURNEY

As you nearing the end of this book, you have developed many of the skills necessary to perform music. It is now time to take your trombone journey to the next level! Find community ensembles, chamber groups, jazz combos, rock bands, or even start a band with your musical friends. The best motivation to continue to improve is to find performing opportunities for you to showcase your new talent!

TOOLBOX

KEY SIGNATURE CHANGES
Music can change key signatures throughout the piece.

TIME IN A BOTTLE
Words and Music by JIM CROCE

Copyright © 1971 (Renewed 1999) Time In A Bottle Publishing and Croce Publishing
All Rights Administered by BMG Rights Management (US) LLC
All Rights Reserved Used by Permission

Tempo
Allegro con brio: Fast, with spirit

Dynamics
fp **Fortepiano:** Play note loudly, then immediately get quieter

NEW NOTE: F

SYMPHONY NO. 5 IN C MINOR, FIRST MOVEMENT EXCERPT
By LUDWIG VAN BEETHOVEN

Scales are the basis of all music. Practicing scales daily is a key component to good musical technique. Make it a goal to memorize all the scales in this book.

NEW NOTE:

F MAJOR SCALE

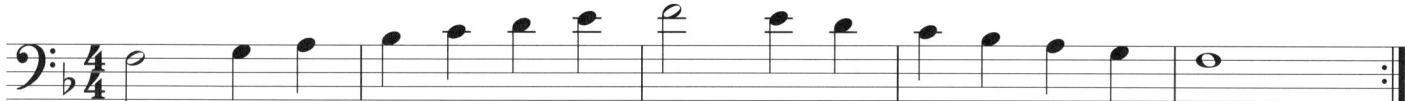

POMP AND CIRCUMSTANCE
By EDWARD ELGAR

Copyright © 2022 by HAL LEONARD LLC
International Copyright Secured   All Rights Reserved

Congratulations, you did it yourself!

ALTERNATE POSITIONS

The higher the range of the note, the closer the partials are together. This creates alternate positions for many notes in the trombone upper range. There may be instances where alternate positions make playing the music easier or more convenient. The first position listed is the most common position, followed by secondary options. Some of the most commonly used alternate positions are bolded in this chart.

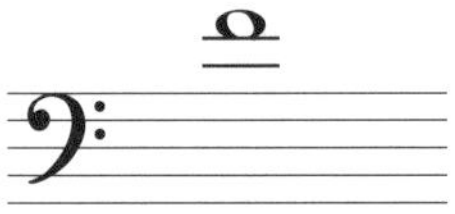

F: 1, **4**, or 6

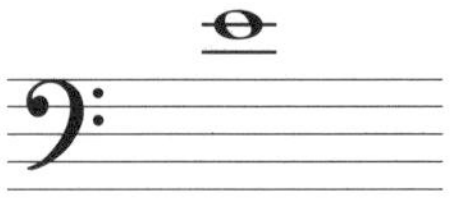

E: 2, 5, or 7

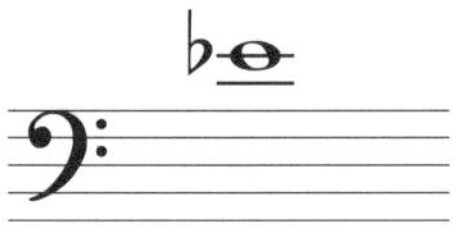

E♭: 3 or 6

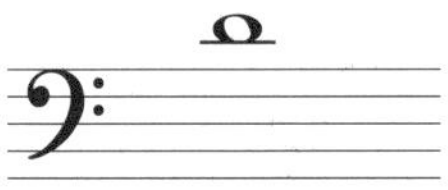

D: 1, **4**, or 7

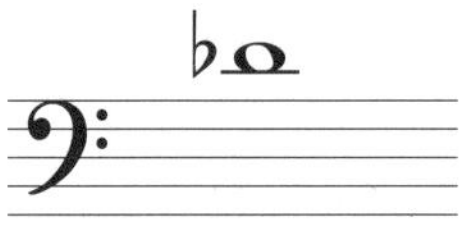

D♭: 2 or 5

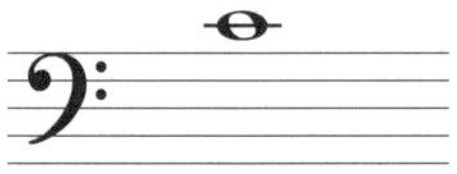

C: 3 or 6

B: 4 or 7

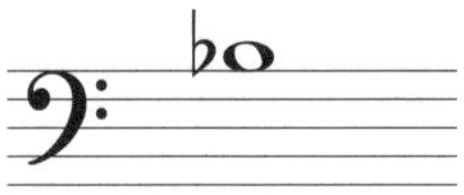

B♭: 1 or **5**

A: 2 or 6

A♭: 3 or 7

F: 1 or **6**

E: 2 or 7

VOCABULARY TERMS

A tempo: return to the original tempo

Accent: an articulation, attack note by playing stronger

Accidental: sharp, flat or natural that appears in a measure

Adagio: slow tempo

Allegro: fast tempo

Andante: slower "walking" tempo

Aperture: the opening that air leaves your mouth and enters the mouthpiece

Articulation: style in which you attack, or tongue each note

Bar line: divides the music staff into measures

Breath mark: indicates where to breathe

Coda: the conclusion

Common time: another way to notate 4/4

Con brio: with spirit

Crescendo: gradually get louder

Cut time: value of each beat from 4/4 is cut in half, also notated as 2/2

Da Capo (D.C.): from the beginning

Decrescendo: gradually get softer

Del Segno (D.S.): from the sign

Dot: adds half of the value of the note

Double bar: indicates new section within music

Dynamics: indicate how loud or soft to play

Embouchure: position of mouth on the mouthpiece

Enharmonic: two notes with the same pitch but written with different note names

Fermata: hold for a longer, unspecified time

Fine: the end

Flat: lowers note a half step

Forte: loud

Fortepiano: play loud, then immediately get quiet

Fortissimo: very loud

Glissando: musical effect in which slide is moved without tonguing

Harmonic series: all notes with the same slide position

Internal repeat: repeat sign at the beginning of a measure

Interpretation: personal changes make to music with tempo, articulation and dynamics

Interval: distance between notes

Intonation: pitch accuracy

Key signature: indicates whether to play the notes sharp, flat or natural

Largo: very slow tempo

Ledger lines: lines that extend the music staff

Legato: an articulation, smooth and connected

Lip slur: playing more than one note in the same position without tonguing

Maestoso: majestically

Marcato: an articulation, "march style" with strong attack followed by decay in sound

Measure: space between two bar lines

Meter: a regular recurring pattern of beats

Metronome: device used to keep steady tempo

Mezzo forte: medium loud

Mezzo piano: medium soft

Moderato: medium tempo

Molto: much

Natural: cancels sharps or flats to return note back to its normal state

Octave: interval that is eight notes apart, both notes have the same name

Offbeat: a beat that does not fall on a strong beat

Partials: the individual notes in one position

Phrase: musical sentence, or complete idea

Piano: soft

Pickup note: note or group of notes that occur before the first full measure

Rallentando: gradually slow down

Ritardando: gradually slow down

Rubato: temporary speeding up and slowing down

Scoop: technique of sliding up to the note

Sharp: raises note a half step

Shuffle: rhythmic feel or groove, first eighth note feels longer than the second

Slur: an articulation, connects two or more notes of any pitch

Staccato: an articulation, light and separated

Staff: lines and spaces where music is written

Subdivision: breaking the beat into smaller, even pieces

Swing: musical style where eighth notes are not even in length

Syncopation: rhythmic change where feeling shifts to the offbeat

Tempo: speed of the music

Tenuto: an articulation, note is held full value

Tie: connects two or more notes of the same pitch together

Time signature: indicates number of beats in a measure as well which type of note receives one beat

Tone: sound produced with the instrument

Triplet: three notes of equal length grouped together

Vibrato: rapid bending of a pitch

POSITION CHART

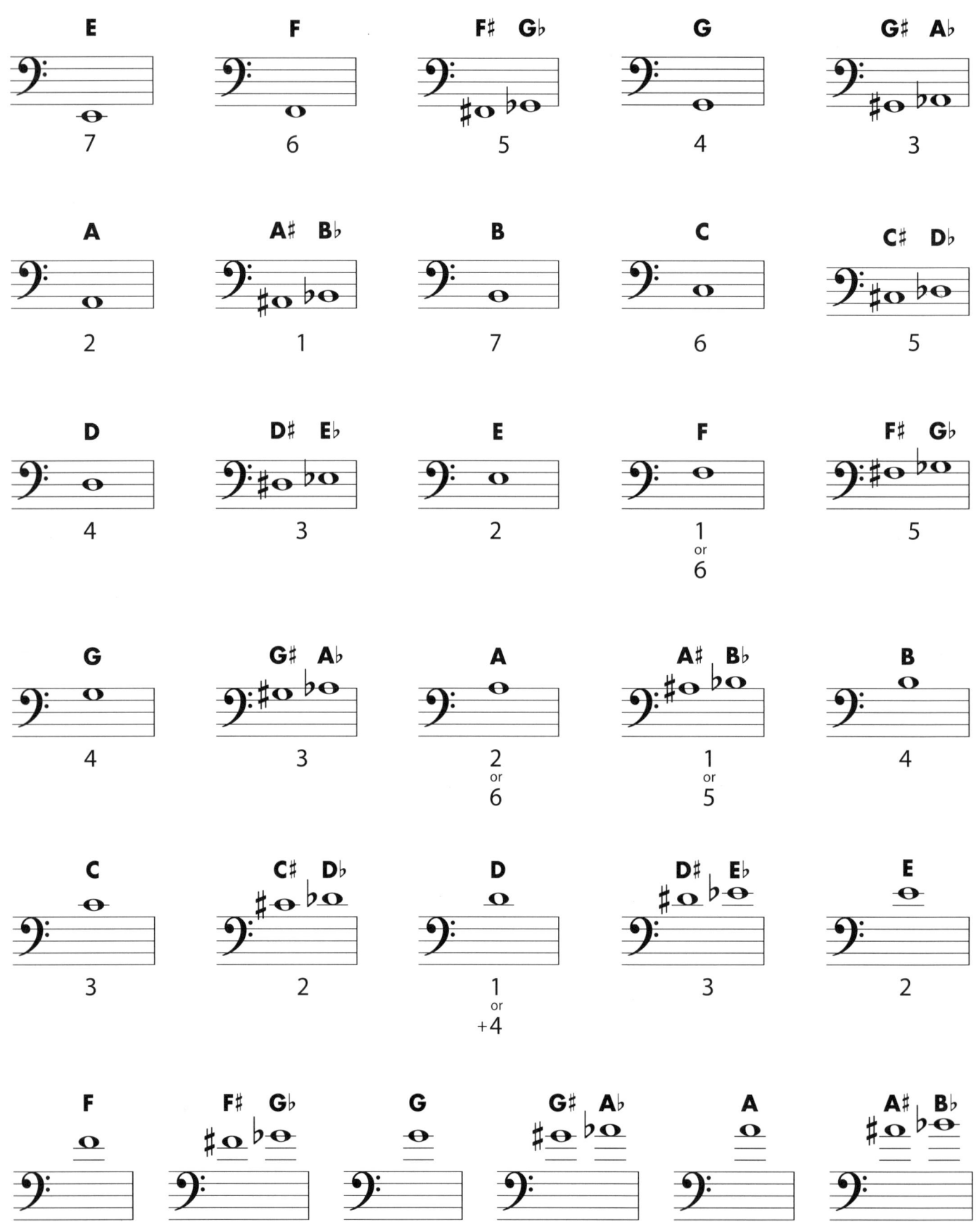

+ = Make the slide a little longer.
− = Make the slide a little shorter.